What readers are saying about
Pragmatic Project Automation

Where has this book been all my life?! Mike Clark's clear, concise, and fun style has me on the edge of my seat eager to find out what trick is next. His CruiseControl RSS publisher is already in action on my projects, and even more of these gems are working their way into my routine. Lava Lamps and Groovy—the hippest software book ever!

> ► **Erik Hatcher**, Co-author of *Java Development with Ant* and *Lucene in Action*

From the minute I learned about the *Pragmatic Starter Kit*, this book was the one I was most eager to read. Now that I've read it, it's the one I'm most eager to recommend.... Mike's book shows clearly that automation is part and parcel of good software engineering: well-designed systems lend themselves to automation, and automation helps us build good systems.

> ► **Glenn Vanderburg**

This book—fun and interesting to read—is a wonderful collection of tips and tricks that will help you take simple everyday tools and do amazing things with them.

> ► **James Duncan Davidson**, Creator of Ant

We've all heard that time is money. So it follows naturally that saving time is saving money. This book shows you how to do both.... I'm going to staple this book to my desk, so it doesn't 'disappear.'

> ► **David Rupp**, Sr. Software Engineer, Great-West Life & Annuity

If your software project is not automated, you are wasting time and money every day, and I can't think of a better, more thorough, or more practical book to get you started on that path than Mike Clark's *Pragmatic Project Automation*.

> ► **Alberto Savoia**, CTO, Agitar Software Inc.

If you've ever hoped to find a technical book that gave solid, usable examples that you can apply in real life rather than just throwing lofty-sounding buzzwords about, then this book is it.... This book will be mandatory reading on all of my projects from this time forth.

▶ **Simon P. Chappell**, Technical Lead, Lands' End, Inc.

This book is both inspiring and informative. I now have no excuses not to automate my projects.

▶ **David Vydra**, www.testdriven.com

Finally! Mike Clark has captured in this book what has taken me years to learn—how to make the computers do the dull repetitive work so that the developers can spend more time solving the REAL problems.... By implementing the simple guidelines presented here, every software project can, in essence, gain another team member.

▶ **Jonathan Julian**, Java Consultant

Doing the things this book describes saves each member of our team hours of grief and frustration every time we do a release. Overall, I think this is an excellent addition to the lineup—it's valuable stuff, and the writing and examples are very clear.

▶ **Greg Wilson**, Hewlett-Packard

Pragmatic Project Automation explains plainly how and why to automate the building, integration, and release of your projects. This book is a must-read for anyone who wants to have their software project succeed.

▶ **Johannes Brodwall**, Senior Software Architect, BBS Norway

In the tradition of the Pragmatic series, *Pragmatic Project Automation* introduces a wealth of techniques (and free tools) for improving both software quality and software developers' quality of life.

▶ **Darin Herr**, Web Developer

Pragmatic Project Automation

How to Build, Deploy, and Monitor
Java Applications

Pragmatic Project Automation

How to Build, Deploy, and Monitor
Java Applications

Mike Clark

The Pragmatic Bookshelf

Raleigh, North Carolina   Dallas, Texas

Many of the designations used by manufacturers and sellers to distinguish their products are claimed as trademarks. Where those designations appear in this book, and The Pragmatic Programmers, LLC was aware of a trademark claim, the designations have been printed in initial capital letters or in all capitals. The Pragmatic Starter Kit, The Pragmatic Programmer, Pragmatic Programming, Pragmatic Bookshelf and the linking "g" device are trademarks of The Pragmatic Programmers, LLC. The configuration of the LAVA® brand motion lamp is a registered trademark of Haggerty Enterprises, Inc.

Every precaution was taken in the preparation of this book. However, the publisher assumes no responsibility for errors or omissions, or for damages that may result from the use of information (including program listings) contained herein.

Our Pragmatic courses, workshops and other products can help you and your team create better software and have more fun. For more information, as well as the latest Pragmatic titles, please visit us at:

> http://www.pragmaticprogrammer.com

Printed in the United States of America.

ISBN 0-9745140-3-9

Printed on acid-free paper with 85% recycled, 30% post-consumer content.

First printing, June 2004

Version: 2004-6-21

Contents

About the Starter Kit

Our first book, *The Pragmatic Programmer: From Journeyman to Master*, is a widely acclaimed overview of practical topics in modern software development. Since it was first published in 1999, many people have asked us about follow-on books, or sequels. We'll get around to that. But first, we thought we'd go back and offer a *prequel* of sorts.

Over the years, we've found that many of our pragmatic readers who are just starting out need a helping hand to get their development infrastructure in place, so they can begin forming good habits early. Many of our more advanced pragmatic readers understand these topics thoroughly, but they need help convincing and educating the rest of their organization or team. We think we've got something that can help.

The *Pragmatic Starter Kit* is a three-volume set that covers the essential basics for modern software development. These volumes include the practices, tools, and philosophies that you need to get a team up and running and superproductive. Armed with this knowledge, you and your team can adopt good habits easily and enjoy the safety and comfort of a well-established "safety net" for your project.

The first volume, *Pragmatic Version Control*, describes how to use version control as the cornerstone of a project. A project without version control is like a word processor without an Undo button: The more text you enter, the greater the risk, as mistakes will be more and more expensive to fix. *Pragmatic Version Control* shows you how to use version control systems effectively, with all the benefits and safety but without crippling bureaucracy or lengthy, tedious procedures.

Volume II, *Pragmatic Unit Testing*, discusses how to do effective unit testing. Unit testing is an essential technique as it provides real-world, real-time feedback for developers as they write code. Many developers misunderstand unit testing and don't realize that it makes *our* jobs as developers easier. There are two versions of this volume: one based on JUnit (for Java), the other based on NUnit (for C#).

This book, *Pragmatic Project Automation*, is the third volume of the series. It covers the essential practices and technologies needed to automate your code's build, test, and release procedures. Few projects suffer from having too much time on their hands, so *Pragmatic Project Automation* will show you how to get the computer to do more of the mundane tasks by itself, freeing you to concentrate on the more interesting—and difficult—challenges.

These books were created in the same approachable style as our first book, and they address specific needs and problems that you face in the trenches every day. But these aren't dummy-level books that give you only part of the picture; they'll give you enough understanding that you'll be able to invent your own solutions to the novel problems you face that we *haven't* addressed specifically.

For up-to-date information on these and other books, as well as related pragmatic resources for developers and managers, visit us on the web at www.pragmaticprogrammer.com.

Thanks, and remember to make it fun!

Dave Thomas and Andy Hunt
June 2004
pragprog@pragmaticprogrammer.com

Preface

They say the cobbler's child is the last to have shoes. It's the same for software developers—we write applications for others but rarely take the time to automate our own processes. This is crazy: if we let our computers do more of the repetitive, tedious, and boring work for us, then not only do we free up our time to do more worthwhile things, we also guarantee more repeatable results.

Rest assured that in this book you won't find the sort of automation used to make backups or process your payroll. This is automation for those of us who are on the hook to deliver working software next week, the week after, and the week after that. To keep that pace, we need to work smarter, not harder. Manual processes of any duration quickly add up to big problems. Automation is the antidote.

This book shows you how to automate your software project soup-to-nuts: from building and testing your code to deploying and monitoring production software. Follow these automation recipes, and your team will eliminate inconsistency, save time, and make life easier for yourselves and the users of your software.

Where to Find the Goodies

Throughout this book you'll find the machinery of automation: shell scripts, build files, configuration files, and even Java code. Some of these are complete listings while others are mere fragments. If you want to run any of the examples or see the complete listing for fragments, just look in the margin. Each example was derived from the filename printed in the margin next to the example itself.

All the examples in this book are available on the web on the *Pragmatic Project Automation* book's home page. Check out http://www.pragmaticprogrammer.com/sk/auto.

Beyond the Book

Throughout this book you'll also encounter automation stories from the field. Folks were kind enough to contribute these stories to share just how automation is helping them on their real-world projects.

Automation takes many forms and can be applied to all sorts of project activities. This book focuses on what we consider to be the core procedures that are ripe for automation on all software projects. But it doesn't end there. So when you reach the end of this book and want more, we invite you to tune in to http://www.pragmaticautomation.com.

On that site your tireless author will post news and content related to all sorts of project automation, including stories you submit from your project!

A Place Called Home

To guarantee the best possible accuracy, I ran all the examples in this book and copied the console output verbatim whenever possible. Thus, the output uses the conventions of the operating system I call home: Mac OS X. Here's an example of how I change to the directory work in my home directory:

```
$ cd ~/work
```

The $ character is the shell (system) prompt. On Unix, the tilde character ~ is a shortcut for the current user's home directory. Unlike Unix-style paths that typically use all lower-case characters, many of the default paths in Mac OS X use mixed case, so the paths may look different on the machine you call home.

All the example files were dynamically inserted into the book when it was built to avoid the perils of copy/paste. Because I use Mac OS X, this means you'll see a lot more Unix shell scripts than Windows batch files. For those of you who call Windows home, you'll find that its shell scripting language is powerful enough to handle the duties of the Unix scripts you'll see here. Alternatively, Cygwin (`http://www.cygwin.com`) is a free POSIX emulation library that makes it possible to run these Unix scripts on Windows.

Typographic Conventions

italic font   Indicates terms that are being defined or are borrowed from another language.

`fixed` or sans font   Computer stuff (filenames, terminal sessions, commands, and so on).

        A warning that the corresponding material is more advanced and can safely be skipped on your first reading.

        "Joe the Developer," our cartoon friend, asks a question that you may find useful.

Acknowledgments

First and foremost, many thanks to Dave and Andy for the privilege of writing the third volume of your starter kit, for imparting your wisdom, and for all the outstanding support you gave me throughout the process. I've been spoiled.

This book wouldn't be nearly as interesting if it weren't for the stories contributed by James Duncan Davidson, Scott Hasse, Bob Lee, Jared Richardson, Alberto Savoia, and Bryce Unruh. Thanks for sharing your brilliant ideas and experiences.

I'm humbled by the number of people who cared enough to spend their free time helping make this book better. My sincere thanks and appreciation go to David Bock for signing on as an early reviewer; Johannes Brodwall for a thorough technical review from Norway; Simon Chappell for so many wonderful quotes that buoyed my spirit at the end of a long journey; James Duncan Davidson for being a steadfast friend and an invaluable sounding board, and for introducing me to this Mac; Jeffrey Fredrick for all your expert help with CruiseControl; Erik Hatcher for always being a pal and for writing the best Ant book on the planet; Stuart Halloway for your friendship and for creating Flow; Darin Herr for offering to buy the book before it was complete; Jonathan Julian for early and enthusiastic reviews that helped shape the book; Chris Morris for exchanging stories by email; Jared Richardson for setting the bar high for scheduled builds; David Rupp for a phenomenal job cleaning up my sloppy grammar; Alberto Savoia for inspiring everyone to light up Lava Lamps on their project; Jason Sypher for listening to my automation rants before I had this pulpit; Andy Tinkham for typing up review comments in the wee hours of the morning; Glenn Vanderburg for always supporting my work, for a comprehensive review even though you didn't have time, and for so many great memories together on the road; David Vydra for your thoughts and online book plugs; and Greg Wilson for your keen insights and for supporting the starter kit. I hope you all see your influence sprinkled throughout this book.

Nicole made writing this book possible. What's really amazing is that she encouraged me to take on this project, knowing full well the cost of being an author's wife. Thank you, my love, for your daily inspiration.

To Mom, Dad, Cris, Tory, and Sayer: thank you for sharing new life and timeless love.

Reading books has always filled me with wonder and contentment. I never could have imagined that I'd have the opportunity to give that gift to others. My profound thanks to Grandma and Grandpa for teaching me to read and for a lifetime of unconditional love. This book is for you.

Mike Clark
June 2004
mike@clarkware.com

Chapter 1

Introduction

This is the book your computer didn't want published. Until now, your computer has had a life of leisure: reading email, displaying web pages, and maybe even compiling Java code. Meanwhile you've been on the treadmill doing repetitive, mundane, and downright boring tasks that take away time from delivering valuable software and seeing your family.

Simply put, this book tells you how to put this thing called a computer to work doing some of that mundane (but important) project stuff. That means you'll have more time and energy to do the really exciting—and challenging—stuff, such as writing quality code. In other words, we'll task computers to do what they're good at, leaving us to do what we do well.

But aside from the obvious efficiency gains, automation also makes our project's procedures consistent and repeatable so that we spend less time debugging problems. How does this play out in real life? Let's start with a story....

1.1 Look Ma, No Hands!

Today we find Fred, our favorite programmer, working on his company's flagship product, the document management system, or *DMS* for short. OK, so "document management system" might be what Fred calls it on his resumé. It's really just a collection of HTML files that can be indexed and then searched. Fred chuckles as he thinks of how much venture capital (VC) money his company could have raised in 1998 just for promoting something by that name.

But it's 2004, and a cool product name and a web site just don't cut it. These days you actually have to demonstrate working software to loosen the VC purse strings. Speaking of which, Fred is in charge of preparing a demo for the venture capitalists tomorrow at noon. There's just one problem: By that time tomorrow Fred will be a few state lines away from the office. In fact, his RV is out in the parking lot right now, gassed up for a trip to the yearly family reunion in Kansas. Just as soon as he adds this last feature, Fred and his family will hit the road.

It Works on My Machine

Fred can already taste the barbecue sauce as he finishes up the last bit of code. He presses the Compile button on his favorite IDE. No errors. Then he runs all his local unit tests, and they pass. So far, so good. Now for the grand finale. Fred checks out the latest version of the rest of the project from the version control system to set up for an integration test. Then he touches off a build by running the project's build script.

WooHoo! The build succeeded. Fred is reminded once again that he's the world's greatest programmer. So he commits his changes, grabs his lunch pail, and races for the elevator. In the morning, all his team needs to do to deploy the demo is run the deployment script. They may even have time for a game of foosball before the venture capitalists show up at noon. Life is good as Fred, the missus, and all the rugrats crawl into the Winnebago and drive out of town.

Somewhere Out on I-70...

Fred has the pedal to the metal as the RV lumbers down I-70 in the dead of night. Just as the kids have dozed off, Fred is startled back into reality by a beep of his cell phone. It's a text message sent from the scheduled build process on the build machine back at the office, hundreds of miles in Fred's rearview mirror. When it woke up and tried to run a build, it failed. Fred grimaces as he reads the error message. In his haste he forgot to check in a new source file.

Fred leaves a voice mail for his faithful teammate Barney, letting him know that he'll need to check in the file before the demo. And then Fred goes back to counting mile markers.

The Next Morning

Barney strolls into the office a tad late the next morning. The whole team had worked hard preparing for the demo all week, so last night they celebrated by downing some brews at the bowling lanes. Checking voice mail is the last thing on what's left of Barney's mind. He'll return phone calls after the demo.

But he can't help but notice the boiling red bubbles in one of the Lava Lamps that the team uses to indicate the build status.[1] Oh no! The scheduled build has failed. When they left work last night, the green lamp was bubbling. "What could have happened?" Barney wonders as he checks the build status web page. It tells him that since the last successful build, one person has checked in code...Fred! The error message says he forgot to check in a file.

Back on Solid Ground

Perhaps it's time for Barney to check voice mail. He listens as Fred sheepishly explains that a local file on his machine needs to be checked in for the build to work. Having checked in the missing file, Barney wants some confidence that everything is in place for the demo. So he forces an independent build on the build machine. He also cranks up the frequency of scheduled builds so that Fred can't get so far away next time before finding out the build failed.

Everything compiles, and the tests pass on the build machine. Barney then runs a script that automatically creates a release branch containing the current versions of all files in version control, builds and tests the release branch, creates a distribution file, and deploys it into the demo web server.

After running the deployment script, Barney clicks through a few pages of the demo to make sure it looks right. Then he takes an early lunch before folks show up for the demo.

---

[1]Don't worry, you'll learn how to light up your own Lava Lamps in Section 6.2, *Getting Feedback from Visual Devices*, on page 130.

Then, Right Before the Demo...

Barney's pager goes off just as he's finishing his brontosaurus burger. The demo site has crashed. How does he know this? Well, Barney has been burned by demos crashing before. And when he has an itch, he finds some way to scratch it.

Before going to lunch, Barney hooked up a simple monitor to the demo web page. It automatically inspects the site every couple of minutes looking for an error message. If it finds one, it notifies Barney by sending him a text page. Fred gets the same text message on his cell phone, but he's up to his elbows in barbecued spareribs.

This time it looks like somebody shut down the database on the demo machine. Thankfully, there's time to straighten that out before the big demo.

A Happy Ending

Today we find Fred, Wilma, Barney, and the whole crew down at the bowling lanes high-fiving over the huge success of last week's demo. They all laugh at themselves for being in the stone age of automation for so long. "1998 called," Fred jokes. "It wants all its manual, repetitive, boring work back."

Sure, Fred learned his lesson about missing files—but more important, he and his team learned to appreciate all the automation that's watching their backs. It was automation that reduced the risk of a failed demo by notifying them early when problems popped up, wherever they were. It was automation (and version control) that saved them time by giving them a consistent and repeatable way to build and deploy their code. They'll prepare for a lot more demos and (if things go well) production releases after this. Automation will pay for itself many times over. That's what this book is all about.

1.2 Types of Automation

In a short amount of time, Fred and his team experienced the three primary types of automation shown in Figure 1.1 on the next page. Let's look at each of those in detail.

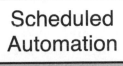

Scheduled Automation	Triggered Automation
Commanded Automation	

Figure 1.1: Types of Automation

- *Commanded automation.* This happens anytime you run a command and the computer performs a set of tasks in a consistent and repeatable manner. For example, Fred ran a build script, and it attempted to generate a build just as it would on any machine. The computer remembered exactly how to do all the build steps for Fred, and everyone else on the project. Likewise, Barney ran a script that carried out the lock-step instructions for deploying the application consistently.

- *Scheduled automation.* Once you can get automation by running a command, then you can put that command on a schedule so that nobody *has* to run it manually. Fred forgot to check in a file, but even though he was miles away the scheduled build ran on time and notified him of the problem.

- *Triggered automation.* Commands can also be automatically run when some important event happens. For example, every time a file is checked in to version control a formatting script could be automatically run. Triggered automation is frequently associated with a scheduled task. For example, Barney wanted to reduce the risk of the demo site not being ready, but he didn't have time to continuously check the site. So he ran a monitor that periodically watched the site for an error event that then triggered his pager.

Because the team made effective use of all three types of automation while preparing for the demo, they got feedback at each of the stages: building, deploying, and monitoring their software. Imagine how stressful it might have been for the team otherwise.

1.3 Questions About Automation

Before diving into automation, it's only natural to have questions. Let's look at some common ones.

What Do I Need to Get Started?

The automation techniques used on Fred's project were fairly simple and inexpensive, but they didn't come for free. The team needed a few basic things in place before they could capitalize on automation.

- *Version control.* A central repository for all the files in their project gave the team a place to synchronize all their work. This in turn gave the build machine a single source from which the project could be built. Using version control also allowed Barney to create a snapshot of all the files used to build the demo so that the same demo can be reproduced at any time in the future. Version control is covered in detail in [TH03].

- *Automated tests.* Running automated tests—tests that check their own results—gave the team confidence in their code base. Fred ran automated tests on his local machine before checking in code to version control. The tests also ran as part of the scheduled build on the build machine to check that all the project code worked in harmony. Barney then ran the same automated tests to verify that the code in the release branch was ready for distribution. At each step in the project life cycle, from writing code to deploying a new release, the automated tests were run to gain confidence before moving on. Indeed, automated tests are the underpinning of effective project automation. Writing good automated tests is covered in detail in [HT03].

- *Scripting.* The team needed to write a few shell scripts (or batch files) to train the computer how to automate procedures. And while you can use programming languages such as Java for automation, a simple shell script is quicker to write, simpler to debug, and doesn't require a build process. Throughout this book we'll look at several scripting examples that make it easy for beginners to follow along.

- *Communication devices.* Automation helped the team communicate and get feedback even while they were on the go. Email and web pages are standard communication tools on software projects, but all too often they get ignored. It was a Lava Lamp that captured Barney's attention. Cell phones and text pagers let you get notifications on the road (or at the beach). Thankfully, we're surrounded by such communication devices these days, and in this book we'll put them to good use.

Why Should I Automate Something?

Frankly, you've got better things to do than piece together builds, follow checklists full of release commands, copy files around on servers, and monitor running programs. So automation will give you back something you don't have enough of: time. And with the global competition for development work heating up, you have to be as productive as possible.

Better yet, automation will give you confidence because automated procedures are accurate, consistent, and repeatable. People just aren't as good at repetitive tasks as machines. You run the risk of doing it differently the one time it matters, doing it on one machine but not another, or doing it just plain wrong. But the computer can do these tasks for you the same way, time after time, without bothering you. You don't have to fear something bad happening when you hit the Enter button.

Automation also reduces the need for documentation. Rather than explaining to a new team member all the steps that go into making a build or generating a release, you just show her how to run a script. And if she's interested, the script has all the details.

Automation changes the way you work. Not only does it make your job easier, it also enables you to perform critical project procedures as often as you should.

When Do I Automate Something?

The simple answer is that you should apply automation whenever you've grown tired of doing something manually. Some folks have higher boredom thresholds than others. As a rule of thumb, manual procedures that will be run more than twice should be automated. Odds are the third time won't be the last.

Errors follow naturally from boredom, so if a repeated manual procedure needs to be accurate and consistent, then it's time for automation.

But remember, this book is about being pragmatic. Never spend more time developing an automated solution than the time the solution will ultimately save.

When Should Automation Run?

The frequency of automation varies with the procedure being automated. For example, the build process is commanded automation that runs whenever we want to create a build. Scheduled builds, on the other hand, should run as often as necessary to give us timely feedback about the health of our software. The scheduled build we'll set up will run many times a day.

Releasing and deploying applications will occur on a less frequent basis, in phase with the project's release cycle. When we have enough new features or bug fixes, we run a command to generate a release and possibly another command to deploy new software to a server.

Monitoring can happen in real time such as when an event is triggered or in a polling loop with a configurable interval.

In the road map that follows, each procedure we automate includes a suggestion of its frequency.

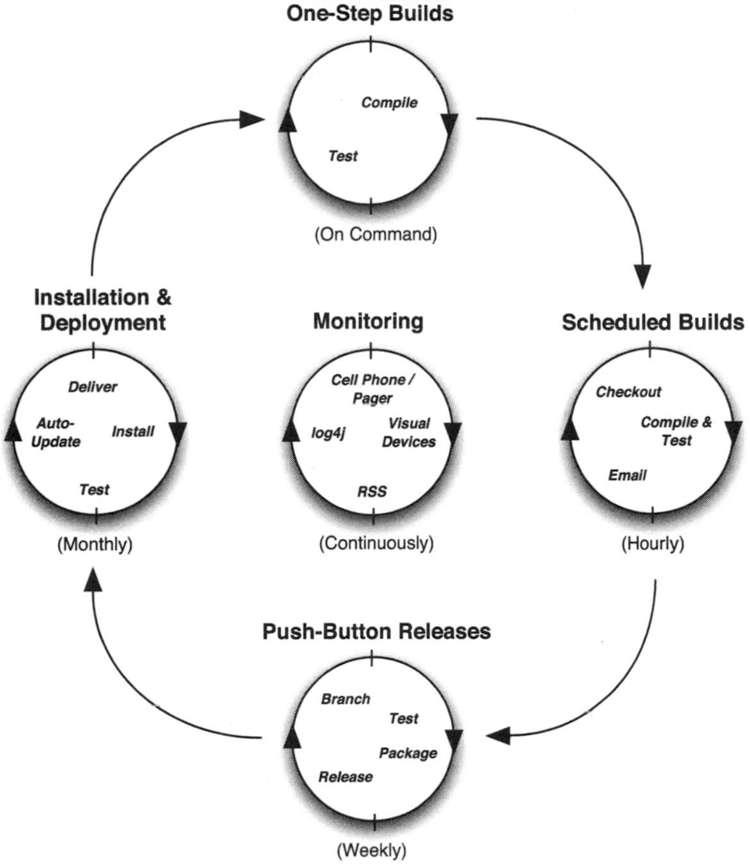

One-Step Builds

Compile

Test

(On Command)

**Installation &
Deployment**

Deliver

Auto-
Update   Install

Test

(Monthly)

Monitoring

Cell Phone /
Pager

log4j   Visual
Devices

RSS

(Continuously)

Scheduled Builds

Checkout

Compile &
Test

Email

(Hourly)

Push-Button Releases

Branch

Test

Package

Release

(Weekly)

Figure 1.2: AUTOMATION ROAD MAP

1.4   Road Map

Figure 1.2 shows the procedures we'll visit. We'll start with one-step builds that can be run by everyone on your team. Then we'll put the build on a schedule so we always have fresh software. When it's ready to be released, we'll push a button to cut a new distribution. Finally, we'll make that distribution available to our customers through an automated installation process. Throughout this cycle we'll set up monitors that alert us to problems that require our attention.

Chapter 2

One-Step Builds

Let's dive right in by automating a procedure that gets run repeatedly by programmers: building and testing code.

2.1 Building Software Is Like Making Sausage

When you sit down and write a computer program, you're creating something unique. It's a human process that involves elements of art, craft, science, and engineering. Try as you may, you just can't bottle up a programming session and replay it later. Therefore, *writing* software isn't anything like the mechanical process of making sausage.

Building software, on the other hand, is a lot like making sausage. For starters, it's messy. You really don't want to know how your beautiful source code is ground into bits to be consumed by a computer. It's also a repeatable process: every time you run a build, you get a consistent copy of your unique program.

The Build Process

To "bake" a build you first need a recipe—commonly referred to as the *build file*. The build file lists all the ingredients that *build file* go into baking the build including source files, configuration files, and vendor libraries. The build file also includes step-by-step instructions for mixing those ingredients together into something tasty. We either write the build file from scratch or, like any great recipe, it's handed down to us from other programmers.

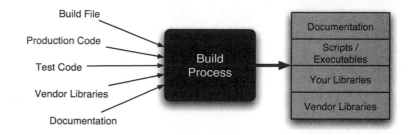

Figure 2.1: THE BUILD PROCESS

build process

A *build process* is nothing more than a series of steps that transmogrify our creative artifacts into a software deliverable. In other words, a build process simply follows the instructions in our carefully prepared build recipe. It takes the ingredients as inputs, turns the crank a few times, and pops out software packaged ready to use. Indeed, it's the build machinery inside the black box at the center of Figure 2.1 that affords us more time for the software writing process.

Making CRISP Builds

Having an automated build process lets us mass-produce our software at the push of a button. If you need to change how the software is put together, alter the recipe and push the button again. Otherwise, automation lets you ignore the recipe.

But being able to push a button to generate a build is as much about consistency as it is about efficiency. That is, a one-step build process lets us make builds that are CRISP.

- Complete
- Repeatable
- Informative
- Schedulable
- Portable

Let's look at each quality of a CRISP build in turn.

Complete Builds

Complete builds are made from scratch using only the ingredients specified in the build recipe. That is, you don't want to spoon-feed files to the build process before it runs or supplement it with additional files after it has run. These sorts of manual steps are error-prone and easy to forget. And frankly, you've got better things to do than chase down build dependencies every time you run a build.

If the build process is self-sufficient, we can automate it to get a complete build every time the process is run.

Repeatable Builds

The key to producing repeatable builds is to store the build file and all the build inputs in a version control system, such as CVS.[1] This gives you a time machine that allows you to build any version of the software by checking out files using a time stamp or a build label. Given the same recipe and ingredients from any moment in time, this computer will bake an identical build.

A repeatable build is also consistent. This means you can easily regenerate prior software releases if you need to diagnose problems reported by customers, or if you simply want to backtrack.

Informative Builds

Informative builds radiate valuable information to us so that we always know the health of our software. As detectors of unexpected changes, automated tests play a crucial role in this feedback loop.

If the build succeeds, we gain confidence that what we're building today actually *works*—all the code compiled, all the tests passed, and all other build artifacts were produced without error. By knowing that everything works today, and each subsequent day, we don't have to cross our fingers and hope that it all works the day we try to deliver.

---

[1] http://cvshome.org

If the build fails, we want to know quickly why, so we don't spend a lot of time debugging what went wrong. An informative build provides detailed information that points to the source of any failure: a required file that's missing, a source file that didn't compile, or a test that failed.

Schedulable Builds

By making builds complete and repeatable, we effectively have a build that can be run on a schedule. Since everything that goes into making a build is available in the version control system, a computer can easily generate fresh builds many times per day or on demand whenever we want.

A scheduled build can occur at a specified time of day (e.g., midnight), on a time interval (e.g., every hour), on an event (e.g., when we check source code in), or one after another continuously. And the beauty of it is we don't have to do anything. The builds get done in the background while we carry on coding.

Portable Builds

Last, but certainly not least, portable builds can be baked in any reasonably well-stocked kitchen. It's the recipe and ingredients that matter, not the features of the oven. Not only can we make a build whenever we want, we can make it *wherever* we want.

A portable build doesn't necessarily mean you should be able to build a Unix application on a Windows box. Rather, if the application builds on a Unix machine, then it should be easy to build the application on *any* Unix machine. Likewise, running a build shouldn't be dependent on any particular IDE, a machine's IP address, or the directory from which it's run.

All this talk of baking must be making you hungry. So let's don our chef's hat and bake a CRISP build. We'll start by defining our project directory structure.

The Compile Button Isn't a Build Process

As appealing as it might be to use it as such, the Compile button on your favorite IDE isn't a build process that generates CRISP builds. An IDE is a powerful development tool for compiling code, browsing its structure, and even refactoring code efficiently. However, on Java projects everyone seems to use their personal favorite IDE. If you have your build process locked up behind an IDE button, then that means the whole team has to agree on the *right* IDE. Good luck with that.

And even if everyone could agree on an IDE (or you let the winner of an arm-wrestling match decide the standard IDE), everyone on the team needs to configure their installation identically so that everyone gets consistent builds. You could put the IDE's configuration files under version control so that everyone on the team shares the same configuration—this takes discipline, but it can be done.

Now how do you automate the build process on a schedule? Do you park a programmer in front of the IDE to push the Compile button whenever a food pellet appears? Well, we're programmers, so we could write a script that launches the IDE and pushes the button for us. But that's not what the IDE is designed for, and running builds this way makes integration with build-scheduling tools more difficult.

You get more flexibility by externalizing the build process from any particular kind of IDE. This gives anyone, regardless of their IDE affiliation, the freedom to run a build manually or to configure a build to be run unattended. And by having a canonical build process, you don't sacrifice build consistency in the name of flexibility. Fortunately, the new generation of Java IDEs are moving toward using standard build systems such as Ant, which we'll explore a bit later. This allows you to run the same build process from inside the IDE as you do outside the IDE.

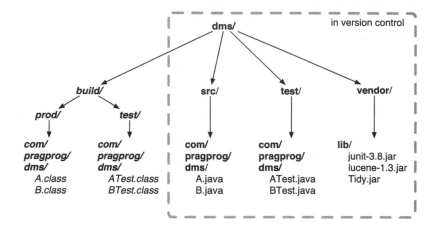

Figure 2.2: PROJECT DIRECTORY STRUCTURE

2.2 Choosing a Project Directory Structure

Before you can start making builds, you need to lay out a directory structure for the project. These directories will contain the inputs to the build process and store its outputs.

And not a moment too soon, the marketing department has returned from an extended off-site meeting where they came up with a name for our software project: the Document Management System (*DMS*). They'll probably change their minds tomorrow, but we need to get started now.

Before marketing has a chance to rethink the name, create a directory called dms as the top of the project directory structure. You have a lot of options for defining subdirectories, but being consistent is more important than choosing the right names. We've had good success automating projects that use the structure shown in Figure 2.2.

Build Inputs

The src and test directories contain the primary build inputs. All the production source files go in the src directory, and the test files go in the test directory. These directories mirror each other using the Java package structure, which means the test files are in the same Java package as the production code they test. It's just easier to keep things organized when you put test code in a separate, but parallel, directory structure.

The production and test source files are the things you're being paid to write, so you need to put the contents of the src and test directories into the version control system.

The vendor directory contains all the third-party libraries that the production code uses. When the build compiles the code, it will need to reference these libraries.

You could easily download the libraries in the vendor/lib directory if you were to lose them, but the source code may be dependent on specific versions of each of these libraries. In the future, you may not be able to find all the correct versions to run a build. Storing the vendor directory and its contents in your version control repository ensures that the build is complete and repeatable.

Build Outputs

When the build runs, it will compile all the Java source files—production code and test code—into class files. Those class files will go in the build/prod and build/test directories, respectively. Again, those directories use the same Java package structure as the source files. Putting the build outputs into separate directories makes it easy to ship only the production class files.

The build directory will only contain files generated by our build process. Given that the build inputs are already under version control, you can consistently regenerate the build outputs. There's no need to store the build directory in the version control system.

2.3 Making Your First Build

Now that you have the build inputs organized in a directory structure, you're ready to create a build recipe that will bake a build using those ingredients.

In the src directory there's a handful of .java files representing production code. In the vendor/lib directory, there are several .jar files containing vendor libraries that the production code uses. The recipe calls for mixing these two ingredients together by compiling the production code referencing the vendor libraries. If all goes well, you'll end up with .class files in the build/prod directory.

Building from the Command Line

The easiest way to mix ingredients and bake a build is from the command line. The command line can be awkward and terse, but being able to fall back on it in a pinch is a useful skill. Let's walk through how we'd follow our build recipe using the Unix command line.

First, navigate into the dms project directory.

```
$ cd ~/work/dms
```

Once in that directory, everything looks familiar because of the consistent directory structure. Next, because the directory build/prod isn't under version control, create it to hold the build outputs.

```
$ mkdir -p build/prod
```

Finally, mix the build inputs together and cook the build using the javac compiler.

```
$ javac -classpath vendor/lib/lucene-1.3.jar:vendor/lib/Tidy.jar
    -d build/prod src/com/pragprog/dms/*.java
```

There's a lot happening here, so let's take it one option at a time. The -classpath compiler option lists all the vendor JAR files that the production code uses. On Unix, each classpath entry is separated by a colon. This turns out to be a minor annoyance for Windows users, since the classpath separator is a semicolon on that platform. We'll address that a bit later.

The -d option tells the compiler to put the resulting class files in the build/prod directory. Following that, the compiler needs the collection of source files it should attempt to compile. We eagerly give it our whole pile of production source code.

Behind the scenes, javac generates the following files:

```
build/prod/com/pragprog/dms/HtmlDocument.class
build/prod/com/pragprog/dms/Indexer.class
build/prod/com/pragprog/dms/Logger.class
build/prod/com/pragprog/dms/Search.class
```

Believe it or not, you just ran your first build process. It took all the build inputs, ground them through the compiler, and generated the build outputs.

Scripting the Command Line

You'll bake lots of builds before the project is over. If you have to type in all those commands every time you want a build, then you're not going to run many builds. And when you absolutely have to run builds, chances are you'll type in something incorrectly and have to debug what went wrong. You could avoid all this by delegating running a build to someone else on the team, but you'd have to explain to them how to run a build on the command line. So the command-line build process isn't repeatable, at least not in the consistent, always-accurate way we're shooting for.

Equally troubling is that the command-line build process isn't portable. For example, you'll have to remind Windows users that classpath entries are separated from each other by semicolons, not colons. It's a minor matter now, but it will get worse as the build process gets more complex.

You could solve both of these problems by putting the build commands in both a shell script and a batch file (for Unix and Windows users, respectively). Being able to group multiple commands together in a single executable file means that those commands can be repeatedly, and consistently, run by pressing the Enter key. For example, instead of remembering the syntax for several commands, you can bottle up those micro commands in a script and simply remember one macro command, like this.

```
$ sh compile.sh
```

Then anybody with a pulse could create a build by running the appropriate file for their operating system. That's *commanded automation* at work, and for small projects a simple build script might just be enough. But projects rarely stay small. We'll likely need to expand the build process to include steps in addition to simply compiling source files. On Java projects, the build tool of choice is Ant.

2.4 Building with Ant

Ant[2] is an open-source build tool that's specialized for building Java projects. If you run in Java circles, you need to know your way around Ant. And given that our *DMS* project is written in Java, now is a perfect time to put Ant to the task.

What Ant Does for Us

Using Ant offers several benefits over the command-line or scripted build process.

- Ant build files are portable. When you run a build file, Ant will resolve any platform dependencies such as how to format the Java classpath correctly for the underlying operating system. It also knows how to execute a generic command, such as making a new directory, by invoking the appropriate operating-system command. This is a boon because everyone on the team can use one common build file, including a dedicated build machine.

- Ant tracks file dependencies. This means that, for example, it invokes the javac compiler only when a source file has been changed. Thus when you run the compile step, you don't have to wait for *everything* to be recompiled.

tasks

- In addition to knowing how to compile Java source files, Ant includes a comprehensive set of *tasks* that do various and sundry things. For example, Ant includes a task for running JUnit tests. You can also extend Ant by writing custom tasks in Java. For a comprehensive tour of everything Ant can do, see [HL02].

The benefits of using Ant come at a price: You have to express the build recipe in an XML file. The price of admission is arguably worth the support and portability we get out of using a well-known format. But all those XML angle brackets can blur what's really going on, so as we write the Ant build file we'll focus on one section at a time.

---

[2]http://ant.apache.org

> ### NAnt
>
> If you're developing code for Microsoft's .NET platform, we've got some good news: You can follow along in this chapter by using NAnt (`http://nant.sourceforge.net`). It uses a syntax similar to that of Ant (thus the name), so our discussion of Ant here should be easily transferable to NAnt. NAnt's also an alternative to using the treacherous Compile button in Visual Studio to create a build.
>
> Microsoft is also planning to bundle MSBuild, its XML-based build tool, with the next version of Visual Studio ("Whidbey"). At the time of this writing, the MSBuild syntax appeared to be very similar to Ant/NAnt. If Visual Studio will generate MSBuild files for external use, as reported, then MSBuild will be a major step in helping create an automated build process that's also supported in the Visual Studio environment.

Writing an Ant Build File

The easiest way to start using Ant is to write a build file that contains the build steps you typed in at the command line. By default, when Ant is run, it will look for a build file named build.xml in the current working directory. We'll work through writing a build.xml file one section at a time. Figure 2.3 on page 26 shows the complete file.

Define the Project

Open your favorite text editor, and create a build.xml file in the root dms project directory. The first line says that what follows is XML. Then, on the second line, define the project.

```
<?xml version="1.0"?>
<project name="dms" default="compile" basedir=".">
```

An Ant build file defines one *project*. Name your project using the name attribute of the *<project>* element. Setting the value of the `default` attribute to `compile` tells Ant that when you type ant on the command line (giving no other parameters), it should run the `compile` step of the build process. We'll define

project

that step a bit later. Setting the `basedir` attribute's value to
. tells Ant that any other paths used in this build file should
be relative to the directory that contains the build.xml file.

Select the Ingredients

property

Next, you make Ant aware of the project directory structure
by defining a *property* for each of your project directories.

```
<property name="build.dir"      location="build"/>
<property name="build.prod.dir" location="${build.dir}/prod"/>
<property name="build.test.dir" location="${build.dir}/test"/>
<property name="doc.dir"        location="doc"/>
<property name="index.dir"      location="index"/>
<property name="src.dir"        location="src"/>
<property name="test.dir"       location="test"/>
<property name="vendor.lib.dir" location="vendor/lib"/>
```

Each <*property*> element associates a name with the directory in the corresponding `location` attribute. The directories
pointed to by the `location` attributes are relative to the value
of the `basedir` attribute defined in the <*project*> element.

Using Ant properties to name relative directories has two benefits. First, it means that your build file can be run from any
directory. When Ant runs the build file, it will locate all the
directories relative to the directory that contains the build.xml
file. The second benefit is that properties make your build
file easy to maintain. Instead of referring to the build directory, for example, use the `build.dir` property. Then later if
you decide to change the name of the actual build directory
to classes, you need to change only the value of the `loca-
tion` attribute of the `build.dir` property. Everywhere you
reference the `build.dir` property in the build file will then
automatically point to the new classes directory.

This is an example of the DRY principle.[3] Rather than scatter
this crucial build information throughout the build file, we
should define it in one place. Our build script is software, too,
so we should try to design it well, and good design usually has
benefits that you can't foresee.

---

[3]DRY stands for "Don't Repeat Yourself." It's a key software design principle explained in [HT00].

Mix the Ingredients

To generate complete builds, we need to make it easy to specify all the build ingredients. When a dependency on a vendor library creeps into the software, for example, your build process needs to be flexible enough to make adding that ingredient to the build easy. If it's too difficult or time-consuming to correctly specify build dependencies, then no one will bother. The next time the build runs, it will fail because the recipe is missing a key ingredient. And before long, half-baked builds become acceptable, and even expected.

We'll start with the classpath. Following the properties section, define a path that represents your project's Java classpath.

```
<path id="project.classpath">
  <pathelement location="${build.prod.dir}" />
  <pathelement location="${build.test.dir}" />
  <fileset dir="${vendor.lib.dir}">
    <include name="*.jar"/>
  </fileset>
</path>
```

The *<path>* element creates a path named `project.class-path`. We'll use this path later during the compile step of the build process.

First, the two build directories are added to the path using *<pathelement>* elements so that the Java compiler can find all of the class files. Then, using the *<fileset>* element, all the vendor .jar files are added to the path so that the Java compiler can find the vendor classes our classes use. Notice that we use properties when referring to directory names to keep the build file flexible.

By defining a classpath in the build file, the build is self-contained. In other words, you don't have to set up a CLASS-PATH environment variable on every machine that will run the build. If you need to add or update a vendor library that the project depends on, simply drop the file into the directory `vendor.lib.dir` and let the *<fileset>* add it to the classpath dynamically. This helps us keep the build complete.

Set the Table

target

Next we define the first build step—called a *target*. This target simply creates the directories where the compile step will put the Java class files.

```
<target name="prepare">
  <mkdir dir="${build.prod.dir}"/>
  <mkdir dir="${build.test.dir}"/>
</target>
```

A target is simply a named build step that defines a series of *tasks* to be run in the specified order. The prepare target uses the <*mkdir*> task to create the build output directories. This is equivalent to using mkdir on the command line, but it works on any operating system, doesn't fail if the directory already exists, and makes parent directories if necessary.

Turn the Crank

At long last, we define the compile step. It compiles all of the production source files, putting the resulting class files in one of the directories created by the prepare target.

```
<target name="compile" depends="prepare">
  <javac srcdir="${src.dir}" destdir="${build.prod.dir}">
    <classpath refid="project.classpath" />
  </javac>
</target>
```

The order in which the targets are run is important. That is, you can't compile the source files until you have a directory to put them in. You specify order by creating dependencies between targets using their depends attributes. The value of this attribute is a comma-separated list of target names.

For example, the compile target uses the depends attribute to declare a dependency on the prepare target. This means running the compile target will first run the prepare target to create the required directories before compiling any source files. This is a big advantage over using a shell script or batch file that always runs commands sequentially.

After the prepare target has run, the compile target invokes the Java compiler by running the <*javac*> task. The compiler takes all the Java source files in the directory pointed to by the src.dir property and generates the corresponding class files in the directory pointed to by the `build.prod.dir` property. What's more, it's smart about what needs to be compiled because Ant watches the time stamps on the Java source files; you don't have to always recompile everything from scratch.

The `project.classpath` path comes in handy in the compile step. The compiler needs a classpath to find all the vendor JAR files that the source files reference. The *<classpath>* element tells the compiler to use the classpath represented by the value of the `project.classpath` path. We'll use this path again later when testing the build.

Save the Recipe

Figure 2.3 on the following page shows the contents of the build.xml file at this point. Before actually firing up a build, there's one more thing you need to do: Put build.xml under version control. After all, it will be used by everyone on the team, and its contents may change over time. If, a year from now, you check out the project as it is today, you'd want to see today's version of build.xml too.

We've written quite a bit of XML just to compile a few Java source files. Thankfully, most of this text is boilerplate across Ant build files. That's not much consolation, but the upside is once you get the hang of this basic file you'll be well on your way to reading almost any Ant build file. More important, with this build file as a template you can quickly add new steps to the recipe.

Running the Build

Now that you have an Ant build file, running the build is easy. First, navigate into the directory that contains the build.xml file.

```
$ cd ~/work/dms
```

Before running Ant, you'll need to ensure that the ANT_HOME environment variable points to your Ant installation directory and that the $ANT_HOME/bin directory is in your PATH environment variable. Then run Ant from the command line.

```
$ ant
```

```xml
<project name="dms" default="compile" basedir=".">
  <property name="build.dir"       location="build"/>
  <property name="build.prod.dir"  location="${build.dir}/prod"/>
  <property name="build.test.dir"  location="${build.dir}/test"/>
  <property name="doc.dir"         location="doc"/>
  <property name="index.dir"       location="index"/>
  <property name="src.dir"         location="src"/>
  <property name="test.dir"        location="test"/>
  <property name="vendor.lib.dir"  location="vendor/lib"/>
  <path id="project.classpath">
    <pathelement location="${build.prod.dir}" />
    <pathelement location="${build.test.dir}" />
    <fileset dir="${vendor.lib.dir}">
      <include name="*.jar"/>
    </fileset>
  </path>
  <target name="prepare">
    <mkdir dir="${build.prod.dir}"/>
    <mkdir dir="${build.test.dir}"/>
  </target>
  <target name="compile" depends="prepare">
    <javac srcdir="${src.dir}" destdir="${build.prod.dir}">
      <classpath refid="project.classpath" />
    </javac>
  </target>
</project>
```

dms/build.xml

Figure 2.3: THE BUILD FILE

Ant reads the build.xml file and executes the build steps (targets) in the defined order. Because compile is the default target specified in the build file, the build proceeds as follows:

```
Buildfile: build.xml
prepare:
    [mkdir] Created dir: /Users/mike/work/dms/build/prod
    [mkdir] Created dir: /Users/mike/work/dms/build/test
compile:
    [javac] Compiling 4 source files to
            /Users/mike/work/dms/build/prod
BUILD SUCCESSFUL
Total time: 3 seconds
```

This is your *second* build process. It compiled all of the production source files by executing the compile target, but only after first executing the prepare target to create the build output directories.

You can also run the build file with a specific target. For

Joe Asks...
What About Maven?

Let's face it, most Java projects have a similar build process: Compile some code, bundle up the classes in a JAR file, and generate copious amounts of Java-doc. In turn, most Ant build files tend to have the same boilerplate XML and define similar build targets.

Maven* takes the grunt work out of defining a build process with Ant. Think of Maven as being a project manager that knows its way around Java projects. For example, once you tell Maven where your source files live and the versions of libraries they depend on, it figures out how to execute the compile step. That is, you don't have to write a `compile` target in your Ant build file. That's Maven's job. If required versions of third-party libraries aren't available locally when it runs the build, Maven will download those libraries from remote repositories. And to top it all off, Maven will create a project website with navigation to generated documentation (e.g., Javadoc and test reports).

Maven looks promising because it can give you a common view into projects. Running and maintaining the build is then easier because you don't have to wander around in the details. But the jury is still out on Maven, so until it takes over the world it's important to know how to create crisp builds with Ant. Just like understanding how to compile Java on the command line helps you understand and appreciate how Ant works, understanding how to create builds with Ant will help you understand what's going on inside Maven.

---

*`http://maven.apache.org`

Joe Asks...

When Do I Use make vs. Ant?

For building Java projects, Ant is the right tool for the job because it's a specialized build tool that caters to Java environments. Ant offers a slew of what it calls *tasks* to do such things as compile Java source files, generate Javadoc, assemble JAR files, and run JUnit tests. But once you step outside of those predefined tasks, you're on your own. That's the price you pay for a specialized tool.

make, on the other hand, is a general-purpose tool. You can make it to do just about anything (no pun intended). But depending on what you want it to do, it might require more effort than using a specialized tool. And makefiles aren't as portable as Ant build scripts. That's the price you pay for a general-purpose tool.

If you're doing Java development, using Ant is a no-brainer because it works on multiple platforms and its integration with the Java toolset complements its general-purpose usability.

example, to explicitly run the compile target we ran before, type

```
$ ant compile
```

As the output shows, there's nothing for Ant to do.

```
Buildfile: build.xml
prepare:
compile:
BUILD SUCCESSFUL
Total time: 2 seconds
```

When we first ran the build, it compiled all the Java source files. We haven't changed any of those files since running the build. So Ant sees that the .class files are newer than their respective .java files, and therefore nothing needs to be compiled.

OK, so now we have a smarter (lazier) build process. But

we're still just compiling code. In just a minute, we'll expand the build process to test our code as well. But first, you may be wondering if there's a better build file format than all this messy XML. It's an excellent question, and it's one that Ant's creator wrestled with, as well. So let's take a break to hear James' history lesson.

The Creator of Ant Exorcizes One of His Demons
by James Duncan Davidson

The first version of Ant didn't have all the angle brackets that you see sprinkled all over its build files. Instead, it used a properties file and the java.util.Properties class to define what tasks should be executed for a target. This worked really well for small projects but started breaking down rapidly as projects grew.

The reason it broke down was the way that Ant views the world: A project is a collection of targets. A target is a collection of tasks. Each task has a set of properties. This is obviously a hierarchical tree. However, property files give you only a flat name=key mapping, which doesn't fit this tree structure at all.

I wanted a hierarchical file format that would capture the way that Ant viewed the world. But I didn't want to create my own format. I wanted to use a standard one—and more important I didn't want to create a full parser for my own custom format. I wanted to reuse somebody else's work. I wanted to take the easiest way possible.

At the time, XML was just breaking out onto the radar. The spec had been completed, but only recently. SAX had become a de-facto standard, but we didn't yet have JAXP. I was convinced that XML was going to be the next big thing after Java. Portable code and portable data. Two buzzphrases that go well together.

Even better, since XML viewed data as a tree structure, it seemed like a perfect fit for the kinds of things that needed to be expressed in a build file. Add in that XML was still a hand-editable text-based format, and it seemed like a marriage made in heaven. And, I didn't have to write a parser. The deal was done.

In retrospect, and many years later, XML probably wasn't as good a choice as it seemed at the time. I have now seen build files that are hundreds, and even thousands, of lines long, and, at those sizes, it turns out that XML isn't quite as friendly a

> format to edit as I had hoped. As well, when you mix XML and
> the interesting reflection-based internals of Ant that provide
> easy extensibility with your own tasks, you end up with an
> environment that gives you quite a bit of the power and
> flexibility of a scripting language—but with a whole lot of
> headache in trying to express that flexibility with angle
> brackets.
>
> *(To Be Continued...)*

And that, folks, is how computing history is made. If there's
a lesson in all of this, it's that looking back can give us ideas
for how to go forward. Later on we'll take a brief look at one
approach to combining the power of Ant with the flexibility
of a scripting language, without the constraints of XML. But
right now, we have a build that needs a "taste tester."

2.5 Taste-Testing the Build

We've learned over the years that a successful compile doesn't
mean much. The compiler doesn't give you any indication
whether the code will actually work. You have to test to get
that warm, fuzzy feeling. (If you're new to unit testing with
JUnit, please see [HT03] for guidance on how to quickly get
started writing good JUnit tests.)

We place JUnit tests in the test directory. Without these tests
we'd be afraid to change code for fear of breaking something.
Indeed, without the tests our production code becomes a lia-
bility, so our tests live in the version control repository as
first-class source files.

Compiling the Tests

Start by defining a separate build target in the build.xml file
that compiles the test source files.

```
<target name="compile-tests" depends="compile">
  <javac srcdir="${test.dir}" destdir="${build.test.dir}">
    <classpath refid="project.classpath" />
  </javac>
</target>
```

The compile-tests target is very similar to the compile target defined earlier. It differs in that the *<javac>* task compiles
the test source files in the test.dir directory and puts the

resulting class files in the `build.test.dir` directory. That is, the build input and output directories are different. Notice that we're reusing the `project.classpath` path as the classpath for compiling the test code.

Running the Tests

Next, define a build target in the build.xml file that will run all of your JUnit tests automatically.

```
<target name="test" depends="compile-tests">
  <junit haltonfailure="true">
    <classpath refid="project.classpath" />
    <formatter type="brief" usefile="false" />
    <batchtest>
      <fileset dir="${build.test.dir}"
        includes="**/*Test.class" />
    </batchtest>
    <sysproperty key="doc.dir"   value="${doc.dir}" />
    <sysproperty key="index.dir" value="${index.dir}" />
  </junit>
</target>
```

There's a lot going on in the `test` target, so let's look at it piece by piece.

Define a Test Target

Before you can run the tests, you must compile the test code. The `depends` attribute on the `test` target creates a dependency on the `compile-tests` target just defined.

```
<target name="test" depends="compile-tests">
  <junit haltonfailure="true">
    <classpath refid="project.classpath" />
```

If the build succeeds, it should mean that not only did everything compile, but it also passed all the tests. This gives us confidence to use the build outputs. Setting the value of the `haltonfailure` attribute to `true` will cause the build to fail if any test fails.

Did we mention just how useful that `project.classpath` path turned out to be? We've used it again here to define the classpath for running the JUnit tests.

Display Test Output

Next you tell JUnit where to display its output. Do that by defining an output formatter.

```
<formatter type="brief" usefile="false" />
```

In the <formatter> element, use the brief type to print the name of each test case that runs and its statistics, and more detailed information only when a test fails. The plain type prints a bit more information by default than the brief type. The xml type prints the test results in XML format. Setting the value of the usefile attribute to false prints the test results to the console rather than a file.

Create a Test Suite

At this point you have only a few JUnit tests, but in the coming days you'll be writing a lot more. Thankfully, Ant can find tests in your project directory and run all of them in batch.

```
<batchtest>
  <fileset dir="${build.test.dir}"
    includes="**/*Test.class" />
</batchtest>
```

The <batchtest> task gathers all the tests returned by the enclosed <fileset> element and automatically creates a test suite that contains the tests. Just to be explicit about which classes are JUnit tests, we'll name all our test classes using the *Test.java naming convention. These files will be compiled into the corresponding *Test.class files in the directory named by the build.test.dir property for the <fileset> to find. In other words, using the <batchtest> task means that you don't have to remember to add each new test case you write to a list.

Specify Test Properties

Finally, the tests for the *DMS* project need to know the locations of two directories in order to run successfully. They need to know where to find documents and where to put the result of indexing those documents. We'll pass that information in when the tests are run.

```
<sysproperty key="doc.dir"   value="${doc.dir}" />
<sysproperty key="index.dir" value="${index.dir}" />
```

The <sysproperty> element defines a system property as a key-value pair. These properties are accessible in your test code. For example, to locate the absolute path of the doc directory in the project's directory structure, tests would look up the doc.dir system property sent in when the tests are run. Again, because you're using properties here, you can change the actual directory name without having to change the test code.

Figure 2.4 on the next page shows our Ant build file after adding the test-related targets. Figure 2.5 on page 35 shows a visual representation of the Ant target dependencies generated by Grand[4] into a Graphviz[5] "dot" file. If you know what we're going to tell you to do with the build.xml file, you've been paying attention. Check it in to version control already!

Testing the Build

At this point you've defined all the build targets necessary to compile and run your tests. Now to run the tests, execute the test target.

```
$ ant test
```

Since the test target depends on the compile-tests target, you're assured that all the test code is compiled and up-to-date before the tasks in the test target are run.

```
Buildfile: build.xml
prepare:
compile:
compile-tests:
   [javac] Compiling 3 source files to /Users/mike/work/dms/build/test
test:
   [junit] Testsuite: com.pragprog.dms.DocumentTest
   [junit] Tests run: 2, Failures: 0, Errors: 0, Time elapsed: 0.437 sec
   [junit] Testsuite: com.pragprog.dms.SearchTest
   [junit] Tests run: 2, Failures: 0, Errors: 0, Time elapsed: 0.862 sec
BUILD SUCCESSFUL
Total time: 4 seconds
```

Doesn't that just make you feel good? All the code compiles and works. Being able to run the test target whenever you change code gives you confidence. If you happen to break something that's being tested, the build will fail. Once you get

---

[4]http://www.ggtools.net/grand
[5]http://www.research.att.com/sw/tools/graphviz

```xml
<project name="dms" default="compile" basedir=".">
  <property name="build.dir"      location="build"/>
  <property name="build.prod.dir" location="${build.dir}/prod"/>
  <property name="build.test.dir" location="${build.dir}/test"/>
  <property name="doc.dir"        location="doc"/>
  <property name="index.dir"      location="index"/>
  <property name="src.dir"        location="src"/>
  <property name="test.dir"       location="test"/>
  <property name="vendor.lib.dir" location="vendor/lib"/>
  <path id="project.classpath">
    <pathelement location="${build.prod.dir}" />
    <pathelement location="${build.test.dir}" />
    <fileset dir="${vendor.lib.dir}">
      <include name="*.jar"/>
    </fileset>
  </path>
  <target name="prepare">
    <mkdir dir="${build.prod.dir}"/>
    <mkdir dir="${build.test.dir}"/>
  </target>

  <target name="compile" depends="prepare">
    <javac srcdir="${src.dir}" destdir="${build.prod.dir}">
      <classpath refid="project.classpath" />
    </javac>
  </target>
  <target name="compile-tests" depends="compile">
    <javac srcdir="${test.dir}" destdir="${build.test.dir}">
      <classpath refid="project.classpath" />
    </javac>
  </target>
  <target name="test" depends="compile-tests">
    <junit haltonfailure="true">
      <classpath refid="project.classpath" />
      <formatter type="brief" usefile="false" />
      <batchtest>
        <fileset dir="${build.test.dir}"
          includes="**/*Test.class" />
      </batchtest>
      <sysproperty key="doc.dir"   value="${doc.dir}" />
      <sysproperty key="index.dir" value="${index.dir}" />
    </junit>
  </target>
</project>
```

dms/build.xml

Figure 2.4: THE BUILD FILE WITH TESTS

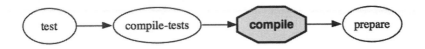

Figure 2.5: TARGET DEPENDENCIES

used to having the safety net of tests, you won't ever want to write code without them.

If tests start failing and you don't fix them right away, then broken tests will quickly become acceptable. Before long, you'll lose confidence in the build. You need to know as soon as possible if the build is failing—that way you can fix it before problems compound or folks start to get the impression that nobody cares. See [HT00] for more details on what happens when "broken windows" go unrepaired.

In the next chapter, we'll keep the build running continuously and publish its status to the team.

2.6 Cleaning Up

After the build process has run, and you know you can reproduce its outputs, you can safely clean up. Just define an Ant target that deletes all the build outputs.

```
<target name="clean">
  <delete dir="${build.dir}" />
</target>
```

The clean target uses the <delete> task to remove the directory referenced by build.dir. This build step is made easier by the fact all the build outputs are placed under a common directory. To clean up, run the clean target.

```
$ ant clean
Buildfile: build.xml
clean:
  [delete] Deleting directory /Users/mike/work/dmo/build
BUILD SUCCESSFUL
Total time: 1 second
```

Now you're right back where you started with a clean project directory. Relax, that's what a good build process gives you: repeatability. Those class files that just went down the drain are merely the by-product of running the build. You can easily reproduce another identical set of class files by running the build process again.

```
$ ant test
```

Since we have all of the target dependencies chained together correctly, that single command runs all the targets in the build file to produce all the build outputs and run all the tests.

```
Buildfile: build.xml
prepare:
    [mkdir] Created dir: /Users/mike/work/dms/build/prod
    [mkdir] Created dir: /Users/mike/work/dms/build/test
compile:
    [javac] Compiling 4 source files to /Users/mike/work/dms/build/prod
compile-tests:
    [javac] Compiling 3 source files to /Users/mike/work/dms/build/test
test:
    [junit] Testsuite: com.pragprog.dms.DocumentTest
    [junit] Tests run: 2, Failures: 0, Errors: 0, Time elapsed: 0.511 sec
    [junit] Testsuite: com.pragprog.dms.SearchTest
    [junit] Tests run: 2, Failures: 0, Errors: 0, Time elapsed: 0.99 sec
BUILD SUCCESSFUL
Total time: 7 seconds
```

Flushing the build outputs was good clean fun, but it actually serves a useful purpose. By defining a `clean` target it's easy to create builds from scratch. It's good to do that once in a while to uncover problems that may be masked by incremental builds. Remember that Ant tracks dependencies by checking the time stamps of files. That's reliable most of the time, but it's possible to get compiled classes out of synch with one another. Running a build from scratch is a sanity check that the build is truly complete and repeatable.

2.7 Scripting a Build

We're going to take a ride on the wild side for a moment. It's certainly deserved after all the hard work you've put into automating the build process. While what follows may not be immediately applicable to your project, it's worth keeping in your back pocket. And enjoy the ride!

Your build process currently uses Ant—a declarative language for describing how to build Java projects. An Ant build file specifies properties and targets. Targets declare a series of tasks to be run and can have dependencies on other targets in the project. This is all you need for most Java projects.

But once in a while, especially when building more complex projects, you might like some conveniences offered by a general programming language. Perhaps you'd like to use a loop to run a task multiple times, each time changing an input value. Or maybe you want only to run a build target based on conditional logic. It's tempting to try to use Ant in these situations because it does have some rudimentary scripting support. But Ant falls short as a scripting language.

This is where we pick up where we left off with the Ant story. James was discussing the historical reasons for Ant's XML syntax, but he goes on to give us a glimpse into the future:

The Creator of Ant Exorcizes One of His Demons (Continued)
by James Duncan Davidson

Now, I never intended for the file format to become a scripting language. After all, my original view of Ant was that there was a declaration of some properties that described the project and that the tasks written in Java performed all the logic. The current maintainers of Ant generally share the same feelings. But when I fused XML and task reflection in Ant, I put together something that is 70–80% of a scripting environment. I just didn't recognize it at the time. To deny that people will use it as a scripting language is equivalent to asking them to pretend that sugar isn't sweet.

If I knew then what I know now, I would have tried using a real scripting language, such as JavaScript via the Rhino component or Python via JPython, with bindings to Java objects that implemented the functionality expressed in today's tasks. Then, there would be a first-class way to express logic, and we wouldn't be stuck with XML as a format that is too bulky for the way that people really want to use the tool.

Hindsight is always 20/20.

As we learned in James' story, scripting languages offer an alternative way of applying logic to the build process. That is, although Ant has some support for scripting, it's not intended to be used as a scripting language. Ant is quite good, however, at handling all the heavy lifting of a build system. And because it's written in Java, it's portable. Ideally, when you need to express logic you'd mix Ant with some scripting glue.

Writing a Groovy Build Script

Groovy[6] is a dynamic scripting language that runs on the Java Virtual Machine (JVM). It uses a Java-like syntax, so as Java programmers we should feel right at home writing Groovy scripts. And Java programmers should feel comfortable picking Groovy because it has traction both with community leaders and with the Java Community Process (JCP).

Groovy also happens to support Ant scripting using Groovy-Markup. That is, you can call Ant tasks right from the comfort of a Java program. Figure 2.6 on the next page shows a Groovy script called build.groovy. The first thing you'll notice is you're not staring at XML angle brackets. Isn't that refreshing? The second thing you'll notice is this looks a lot like Java, but without the type information and semicolons.

The build.groovy script defines a Java class called Build. The last line of the script creates an instance of that class and invokes its compile method. As an example of build dependencies, the compile method first calls the prepare method, which calls the clean method before creating the build output directory.

Then the compile method calls the javac Ant task to compile the source files. It does that using an instance of Groovy's built-in AntBuilder class that knows how to call any of Ant's tasks. The projectClasspath method even uses an Ant fileset to gather up the dependent JAR files.

Running the Groovy Build Script

After installing Groovy, run the build script by typing the following:

```
$ groovy build.groovy
```

---

[6]http://groovy.codehaus.org

```
import java.io.File
class Build {
  srcDir = "src"
  buildDir = "build"
  buildProdDir = buildDir + File.separator + "prod"
  vendorLibDir = "vendor" + File.separator + "lib"

  ant = new AntBuilder()

  void clean() {
    ant.delete(dir: buildDir)
  }

  void prepare() {
    clean()
    ant.mkdir(dir: buildProdDir)
  }

  void compile() {
    prepare()
    ant.javac(srcdir: srcDir,
              destdir: buildProdDir,
              classpath: projectClasspath())
  }

  String projectClasspath() {
    ant.path {
      fileset(dir: vendorLibDir) {
        include(name: "**/*.jar")
      }
    }
  }
}
new Build().compile()
```

dms/build.groovy

Figure 2.6: GROOVY BUILD SCRIPT

The result is standard Ant output.

```
[delete] Deleting directory /Users/mike/work/dms/build
[mkdir]  Created dir: /Users/mike/work/dms/build/prod
[javac]  Compiling 5 source files to /Users/mike/work/dms/build/prod
```

The next time you run this build script, it will compile only the source files that have changed. That's another benefit of continuing to use Ant even as you move toward a scripting language.

Scripting Custom Build Steps

The beauty of scripting the build process with Groovy is that the build file is a regular Groovy program that has access to the Ant build system *and* the JVM. That is, you can use all of

Ant's tasks while enjoying the power of a full-blown scripting language that includes all the familiar Java libraries.

As an example of where scripting comes in handy, imagine you want to loop through all the vendor JAR files and perform a custom action (e.g., instrumenting the class files) on each JAR file. That can be difficult to do with Ant unless you write a custom Ant task that uses a nested *<fileset>*. It's much easier when you have Groovy at your fingertips.

```
void instrumentJARs() {
  scanner = ant.fileScanner {
    fileset(dir: vendorLibDir)
  }
  scanner.each { instrument(it) }
}
void instrument(file) {
  println("Instrumenting ${file}")
  // insert code here
}
```

The instrumentJARs method iterates through all the vendor JAR files using a fileset. For each JAR file, it calls the instrument method, which can perform any processing on the JAR file. The instrumentJARs method can then be called from any step in the build process.

For simple build processes, the benefit of using a scripting language is a wash. But for complex build processes, the scales start to tip back in favor of scripting approaches.[7]

2.8 Getting an Early Start

You might be tempted to delay automating the build until your project has amassed enough code worthy of the automation. Unfortunately, that's usually too late. After you've chosen a project directory structure, the next thing that happens is the programmers settle in writing code. It's what makes a project feel real to us. Those directories quickly start to fill up with code (and tests, of course).

Then one day some programmer pokes his head above the cubicle walls and belts out, "It doesn't build on my machine!"

---

[7]Of course, there are other pure-scripting alternatives, such as Rake (http://rake.rubyforge.org).

Sound the alarm. It's time for a fire drill. After everyone has been rattled from their chairs, some conscientious soul finally wanders over to the hapless programmer's cube for a first-hand look at the disaster.

"Ah, you don't have elmo-2.1.7.jar in your CLASSPATH. Fred just checked in a new file that requires that library."

And then through a flurry of mouse motions, the programmer's IDE gets a clue about elmo-2.1.7.jar and the onerous CLASSPATH is temporarily correct. The crisis is averted, for now, but it won't be long before somebody else incites another fire drill.

The moral of the story is that we save ourselves a lot of trouble by setting up a canonical build process on Day One of the project. Make it the first thing you do after choosing a project directory structure that day, before anyone writes a line of code.[8] Then as the team writes code one file at a time—updating the build file as necessary along the way—the build process will continue to keep everything in check.

What if you already have directories overflowing with source files? Well, thankfully it's never too late to start automating the build. Think of it this way: Every day we postpone automating the build is another day that could be interrupted by a fire drill. And someday (we hope) we'll be ready to release the first version of our software, and many more after that, beyond these cubicle walls. Being able to generate a build at the push of a button will pay for itself many times over.

What We Just Did

We started with a build process that ran from the command line. Then we created an Ant build file that lets everyone on the project run the build in one step. When the build succeeds, it gives everyone confidence that all the code compiles and passes its tests. When the build fails, it provides detailed

---

[8]Megg (http://sourceforge.net/projects/megg) will help you get started quickly by generating a skeleton project directory structure and an Ant build file from supplied templates.

information about what went wrong to save everyone debugging time. This means we're in good shape for scheduling the build. So in the next chapter, we're going to tie our hands behind our back and let the computer run builds for us.

It claims to be fully automatic, but actually you have to push this little button here.

► Gentleman John Killian

Chapter 3

Scheduled Builds

A one-step build process is a gift that keeps on giving. Every time you push the button that runs a build, it will feel like you're getting something for free. This is the beauty of *commanded automation*. Invest just a wee bit of time and get lots of time back. In this chapter we'll take the next automation step: letting a computer push the build button for us.

Scheduled automation takes the one-step build you created and runs it for you, as often as you want, without you ever lifting a finger. You can still run the build manually if you need to, but in the typical case the computer will do it for you. And it turns out that having a machine running builds continuously does more than just save some typing.

Scheduled builds find both integration (compile time) and failing test (run time) problems quickly because they run at regular intervals. For example, if the schedule says to run a build at the top of every hour, then every 60 minutes you'll know if the build is broken. This makes finding problems easier because you have to look only at changes that occurred in that interval. It also makes *fixing* problems easier because little problems don't have a chance to compound into big problems. And because finding and fixing problems is easier, you're less constrained by fear.

How is a scheduled build any different from, say, all the programmers running the build file every few minutes? Well, I don't know many programmers that want to do that. They've usually got better things to do. The build cycle might take a few minutes, or even a few hours, and running it interferes with their work. And even if everyone on the team could quickly run a full build, they might deliberately put off doing so because they have a deadline to meet and they're afraid someone else's changes might conflict and cause delays. That is, unlike a scheduled build, programmers typically only build parts of the system at a time rather than testing that the entire system is integrated.

A scheduled build, on the other hand, has nothing better to do than build and test everything. Once you have a one-step build process, you have much to gain by putting it on a schedule for a computer to run. Thankfully, it doesn't cost much to go this extra mile. It *will* end up costing a lot in the end if you don't start scheduling builds early. So let's get cracking!

3.1 Scheduling Your First Build

Scheduling a build is similar to programming the timer that controls your office building's heating system. You want it to start warming up the place before you're out of bed so that you can arrive to a toasty office. In the same way, you want to come into the office with a nice toasty build waiting for you.

Since you can schedule a build to run at a time or frequency of your choosing, why pick just one time every day? You may as well schedule it to run often so you'll know sooner if your world is collapsing. You want to hear those processors grinding as background noise while you're writing code. It's the sound of software being tested. It's the sound of everyone's time being saved. And that's music to our ears.

Scheduling with cron

The easiest way to schedule a build would be to start by writing a script or batch file that does the following:

1. Checks out the current code from version control.
2. Calls your build file to build and test the code.
3. Squirrels away the build results in a log file.

Next you need to run the build script at some predefined time of day (or night). On Unix, the scheduler of choice is cron. To configure cron, type

```
$ crontab -e
```

This pops open your default editor, the computer's subtle way of asking you what you want it to do and when it should be done. Say, for example, you have a build.sh script that runs your Ant build.xml file. You want cron to run that script at 2 a.m. every morning. To appease cron's cryptic syntax, type the following line into your editor and save the file:

```
0 2 * * * $HOME/work/dms/build.sh
```

Each crontab entry is a single line with six fields. The first five fields represent the schedule, starting from the left: the minute (0–59), the hour (0–23), the day of the month (1–31), the month (1–12), and the day of the week (0–6). A * character in any field means to match all possibilities. For example, using * in the third field means that we want it to run every day of the month. The last field specifies the command to run.

If you're on a Windows box, the built-in scheduler is the at command. To schedule the build.bat file to run at 2 a.m. every morning, for example, type the following at the command line:

```
at 02:00 /every: c:\work\dms\build.bat
```

That's really all there is to it! You just scheduled a build. The computer wakes up about the time most authors are going to bed and runs the build, no questions asked.

Picking the Right Tool for the Job

If cron (or at) gets the job done, then why not just use it and move on? It would feel good to check one more thing off the automation checklist. That's a fair question, especially since this is a book about being pragmatic. Creating a continuous build is less about tools than it is about building continuously. We could start with the simplest tool first, then haul out the commercial-grade tools when, and if, we need them.

There's just one problem: Being pragmatic also means using the right tool for the job. And the simplest tool isn't always the right tool. If you start with a simple shell script such

The Cost of Not Integrating Frequently

It seems that many projects don't have, and claim to not be able to afford, a machine dedicated to automatically building and testing their software on a regular interval. Ironically, these same projects can afford to continuously spend time fighting integration and quality problems.

Just how much programmer time does it take to justify the cost of a dedicated build machine? Consider that on average a ten-person development team costs your company at least $500 per hour. If that team spends merely two hours debugging integration problems over the life of the project, you've paid for a respectable build machine fully capable of compiling and testing code. That's a one-time expense. Then when you start to consider that every day your team is debugging integration problems is another day late to market, you just can't afford *not* to have a dedicated build machine.

A dedicated build machine will help your team conserve time for the really important stuff. If you don't already have one on your software project, then you're behind the competition.

as build.sh, it will likely begin as a few commands: check out the project from version control, run the Ant build file, and redirect the build output somewhere useful.

And then you might decide that emailing the build results to the team would be beneficial to let everyone know how things are going. Better yet, why not publish the build result in HTML for viewing in a browser? Oh, and then you will need a web application that shows all previous build results. Before long you're spending more time maintaining your "simple" script than you are writing production code.

That's where being pragmatic comes in again. If you want a build scheduler with all these fancy features, and you can get it for free, then you should use it rather than spend time creating and maintaining your own scheduler. And if that scheduler is also open source, then you have the option of extending it for any of your special needs later, if necessary.

In that pragmatic spirit, let's take a drive with a scheduler designed to build Java applications. We'll take it one milepost at a time.

3.2 Putting a Build on CruiseControl

CruiseControl[1] is like cron for Ant, but with many bells and whistles. It runs in the background, waking up on cue to run any scheduled Ant targets.

Bear in mind, what CruiseControl does for us isn't rocket science. You could do all this stuff manually if you were bored and didn't mind being pigeonholed as the build guru on your project. It's also nothing a custom build script couldn't do if you wanted to write one and be its maintainer for life. But we're short on time as it is, and maybe even behind schedule. Reinventing all the scheduling features we need that come for free out of the CruiseControl box isn't going to save us any time. CruiseControl isn't the only such tool either, but we'll use it because it meets our needs here.

Choosing a Build Machine

Before installing CruiseControl you need to find a suitable home for it. The machine where you install CruiseControl will be the workhorse for scheduled builds, but it doesn't need to be top-o'-the-line hardware that breaks your bank. You just need it to compile source code and run tests. That's slightly more CPU intensive than reading email and surfing the web, but less so than servicing thousands of concurrent users. If build machines filled out personal want ads, you're looking to hook up with the beautiful bucket of bits described in Figure 3.1 on the following page.

That being said, I realize all the good machines on your project may not be available. If you're lucky enough to find available machines waiting to be put to work, then this decision is easy. Just snag the best one you can and enlist it into service for

---

[1]http://cruisecontrol.sourceforge.net

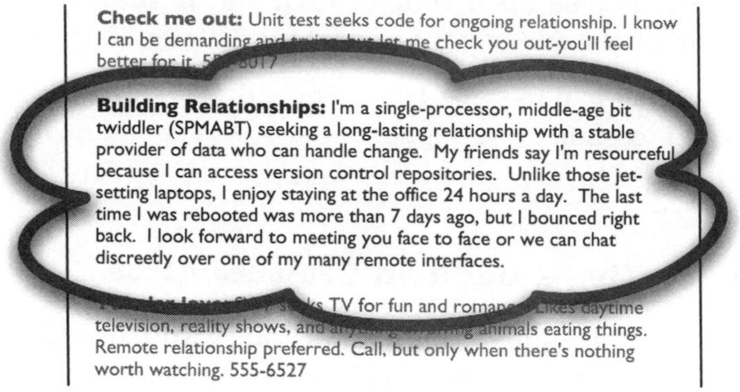

Check me out: Unit test seeks code for ongoing relationship. I know I can be demanding and trying, but let me check you out-you'll feel better for it. 555-9017

Building Relationships: I'm a single-processor, middle-age bit twiddler (SPMABT) seeking a long-lasting relationship with a stable provider of data who can handle change. My friends say I'm resourceful because I can access version control repositories. Unlike those jet-setting laptops, I enjoy staying at the office 24 hours a day. The last time I was rebooted was more than 7 days ago, but I bounced right back. I look forward to meeting you face to face or we can chat discreetly over one of my many remote interfaces.

Regular lover: Seeks TV for fun and romance. Likes daytime television, reality shows, and anything featuring animals eating things. Remote relationship preferred. Call, but only when there's nothing worth watching. 555-6527

Figure 3.1: WANTED: A DREAM BUILD MACHINE

your project. It's happy to be wanted by someone. If you're not so lucky, then consider two-timing with a machine already in service.[2]

And if you just can't find those spare CPU cycles anywhere on your project, then feel free to mention to your manager how inexpensive good hardware is these days. This will go over better than mentioning how expensive programmers are in comparison.

Installing CruiseControl

Now that you've found a suitable build machine, you're ready to introduce it to CruiseControl. This is somewhat like making a new friend only to turn around and offer him a shovel, but trust that we have good intentions here.

When you download CruiseControl, you get a ZIP file. Extract this file into a directory which we'll refer to as $CC_HOME. Then you need to build CruiseControl; on Unix type

```
$ cd $CC_HOME/main
$ sh build.sh
```

---

[2]To temporarily convert a PC into a Linux box without reconfiguring the PC, check out Knoppix (http://www.knoppix.net). It's a Linux distribution that boots and runs completely from a CD. Presto, change-o!

CruiseControl.NET

If you're writing code on the Microsoft .NET platform and using NAnt to build your project, here's another opportunity to follow along. CruiseControl.NET* is a feature port of CruiseControl to the .NET platform. It integrates with the NAnt build tool and the NUnit unit-testing framework. And we'd be remiss if we didn't mention the optional CCTray utility that shows a green or red build status icon in your Windows system tray.

*http://ccnet.thoughtworks.com

Under Windows, the commands are similar.

```
$ cd %CC_HOME%\main
$ build.bat
```

The script then compiles and tests CruiseControl. (Notice that this is commanded automation at work.) When it's done, you'll end up with a file called cruisecontrol.jar in the directory $CC_HOME/main/dist. That file needs to be there to run CruiseControl later.

Preparing a Build Workspace

Next, you need to prepare a workspace on the build machine. This will be the directory from which CruiseControl will run builds and store the results. We'll walk through creating the workspace step by step.

Create the Build Directory

The build workspace is a directory on the build machine. Let's assume we call that directory builds because it's the workspace for all of our scheduled builds. The easiest approach is to create the builds directory in some user's home directory on the build machine. On Unix, log in as that user and type

```
$ mkdir ~/builds
```

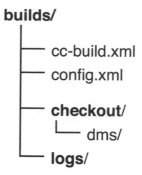

builds/
— cc-build.xml
— config.xml
— **checkout/**
  └── dms/
— **logs/**

Figure 3.2: THE BUILD WORKSPACE

Check Out the Project

So far, we only have one project to build on a schedule: our *DMS* project. It's safely stored in CVS and needs to be checked out locally for CruiseControl to use. To keep the top-level builds directory tidy, check out the dms module into a checkout subdirectory.

```
$ cd ~/builds
$ mkdir checkout
$ cd checkout
$ cvs co dms
```

This assumes that your CVSROOT environment variable is set to the location of your CVS repository. After running these commands the checkout/dms directory will contain all of the files in the dms project. This is a local copy of the project—a snapshot of the project at this instant of time. We'll use this directory just to prime the scheduled build process.

Create a Log Directory

Finally, create a directory that will contain all of the Cruise-Control build log files.

```
$ cd ~/builds
$ mkdir logs
```

Now you have a cozy workspace for scheduled builds. Figure 3.2 shows the directory structure just created. Next, you need to create the cc-build.xml and config.xml files shown in that directory structure. We'll start by writing the cc-build.xml file.

Writing a Delegating Build File

When your scheduled build runs, it should

1. Delete the last build.
2. Check out the current project from CVS.
3. Run the build.

That is, we want to run a "scorch-the-Earth" build. Starting from scratch each time helps avoid the strangeness that inevitably happens with incremental builds. When a build runs successfully from scratch, you get more confidence that it's complete. And if a machine is going to run the build for us, we can afford to be spendthrifts with its time.

You could put those three steps in a target of the existing build.xml file. But it's a good idea to keep the scheduled build procedure separate from the Ant build file used to run builds manually. To do that, create a separate Ant build file called cc-build.xml in the builds directory. The cc-build.xml file just sets up the checkout directory with a fresh copy of code and then delegates the build procedure to the build.xml file.

```
<project name="cc-build" default="build" basedir="checkout">
  <target name="build">
    <delete dir="dms" />
    <cvs command="co dms" />
    <ant antfile="build.xml" dir="dms" target="test" />
  </target>
</project>
```

builds/cc-build.xml

The syntax of this build file should look familiar. It defines an Ant project with build as the default target to run. The basedir attribute points to the checkout directory that contains a local copy of the project.

The meat of the cc-build.xml file is the build target. It first deletes the copy of the project used during the last build to ensure that the next build starts from scratch.

```
<delete dir="dms" />
```

It then checks out a fresh local copy of the project from the CVS repository into the checkout/dms directory.

```
<cvs command="co dms" />
```

This form of the <cvs> task uses the value of the CVSROOT environment variable to locate your CVS repository. Alternatively, you can set the CVSROOT in the cvsRoot attribute of the <cvs> task.

Using the repository as the sole source for the build process means that all the build inputs need to be in CVS. The computer will use the lack of any required file as an excuse for not making good builds. For example, it won't tolerate having to find files littered across the filesystem or the network. Using a version control system also means that any machine with access to the repository is a candidate for running builds.

The build target then needs to call the project's build file to compile and test everything.

```
<ant antfile="build.xml" dir="dms" target="test" />
```

This is where having a one-step build process really pays off. The <ant> task calls the test target of the build.xml file located in the checkout/dms directory.

Test the Procedure

After writing the cc-build.xml file, it's a good idea to test it before handing it off to a cranky computer. To verify the delegating build file works, type

```
$ cd ~/builds
$ ant -buildfile cc-build.xml
```

Make sure to use the -buildfile option here to specify the cc-build.xml file, since by default Ant will look for a file called build.xml. Alternatively, you can use -f as an abbreviation for -buildfile.

Save the Delegating Build File

You need to store the cc-build.xml file under version control so you don't lose it. This presents a slight conundrum because the build file checks out the project from CVS, and yet it's in CVS itself. But cc-build.xml isn't likely to be updated all that often, so just manually check out cc-build.xml into your builds directory whenever it's changed. This is another benefit to using a separate build file for CruiseControl builds, rather than just adding a target to the main build file.

All we've done here is created a wrapper around our existing build file: build.xml is wrapped by the cc-build.xml file. This delegating build file checks out the project and builds it, just as you'd do it from the command line.

Configuring the Build Process

Think of the cc-build.xml file as playing the role of any new programmer on the team. They show up with an empty directory, check out the project anew, and build it with the expectation that everything will work. That is, they provide an objective second opinion as to whether the builds are successful. Unfortunately, no one can hire enough new programmers to get build feedback as often as needed in order to keep working confidently. That's where CruiseControl comes in.

Our next step is to tell CruiseControl how and when it should run our build. By default, it looks for a configuration file called config.xml that defines the projects it's responsible for building. We'll write the config.xml file one section at a time. The complete file is shown in Figure 3.3 on page 59.

Define the Project

Create the config.xml file in the builds directory. The first few lines of config.xml set up the project.

```
<cruisecontrol>
  <project name="dms" buildafterfailed="false">
```

The name attribute of the *<project>* element identifies this project. Multiple projects can be defined in this file with each project having a unique name.

By default, CruiseControl will continue to attempt to build a project even if the build failed on the last attempt and nothing has changed in CVS since then. This can be useful for projects that have dependencies on external resources that might not be available when the build runs: If at first you don't succeed, try and try again. But it's overkill for this project since everything it depends on is in the CVS repository. Set the value of the `buildafterfailed` attribute to `false` so that when the build fails the CPUs will get a chance to cool down while you fix the problem.

Bootstrap the Build

bootstrappers

Next, define *bootstrappers*—things to be done before the build cycle happens.

```
<bootstrappers>
  <currentbuildstatusbootstrapper
    file="logs/dms/currentbuildstatus.txt" />
</bootstrappers>
```

The *<currentbuildstatusbootstrapper>* simply writes a message to the logs/dms/currentbuildstatus.txt file indicating that a build cycle has begun. Running a bootstrapper doesn't mean that a build will be attempted, only that CruiseControl has awakened to check if a build is necessary. Think of it as CruiseControl punching in for work.

Check for Changes

You want to run a build only if something has changed in the CVS repository. After all, there's no sense running builds if all the programmers are away at a conference honing their skills. Next define how CruiseControl checks for changes to determine if a build is necessary.

```
<modificationset quietperiod="60">
  <cvs localworkingcopy="checkout/dms" />
</modificationset>
```

The *<modificationset>* element tells CruiseControl what to watch to see if a build is required. The project is in CVS, so you can use the *<cvs>* element with the `localworking-copy` attribute pointing at the local copy of the dms module.[3] This means that the local directory will be used to locate the CVS repository to determine if something has changed. This keeps you from having to hard-code the CVSROOT in the config.xml file. The important thing to remember is that a build

---

[3]ClearCase, Subversion, StarTeam, Visual SourceSafe, and other version control systems are also supported.

will be attempted only if something being watched by the <*modificationset*> has changed.

CVS doesn't support atomic commits, which means if you check in 10 files they are committed in 10 separate steps. What happens when 5 of 10 changes have been committed when CruiseControl wakes up? It will notice that at least 5 things have changed since the last time it looked at the repository. But starting a build at this point would be problematic because not everything has made it into the repository.

To give you a chance to get everything checked in before a build starts, set the value of the <*modificationset*> element's `quietperiod` attribute to 60 seconds. This means the CVS repository must be quiet (inactive) for 60 seconds before a build is attempted. If CruiseControl wakes up and detects that changes have been made to the repository during the quiet period, it will go back to sleep and check again later.

Dial In the Build Interval

Finally, define the build interval and how a build should be attempted.

```
<schedule interval="60">
  <ant buildfile="cc-build.xml" target="build" />
</schedule>
```

The <*schedule*> element tells CruiseControl *when* to attempt a build. Here, we set the `interval` attribute to 60 seconds. This means CruiseControl will wake up every minute to check to see if any changes have been made as indicated by the results of the <*modificationset*> element. In other words, the dms module of CVS will be polled every minute for differences. If changes were made, but not within the quiet period, then a build will be attempted.

The <*ant*> element tells CruiseControl *how* to run a build. In this case, we want it to invoke the `build` target of our delegating build file—cc-build.xml. Recall that this build file will delete the last build, check out a fresh copy of dms from CVS, and then run the `test` target of the checkout/dms/build.xml file.

To recap what we've done here: Every minute CruiseControl will check to see if something in the project has changed. If

> ```
>  \ /
>  °˘  Joe Asks...
>  ˘
>        How Frequently Should a Build Run?
> ```
>
> The only limiting factor to how often you can run the build is the length of your build cycle. Some projects may not even finish the compile step in under a minute. But if we can build the entire project in less than five minutes, for example, then why not build every five minutes?
>
> Remember, if nobody changes code, the build just doesn't run. But if somebody does change code, then wouldn't it be nice to know as soon as possible if all of the tests still pass? If they didn't pass, then you'd only have to look at the last five minutes worth of changes to diagnose what went wrong.
>
> On a real-world project you'll probably have different types of tests: unit tests, acceptance tests, performance tests, etc. You don't want to wait for all of those tests to run just to see if your unit tests passed. To avoid that, each type of test would have a different Ant target and you'd configure CruiseControl to run each target on a different schedule.
>
> Schedule build targets to run based on how often you want feedback about your system. For example, you might run all the unit tests every five minutes, all the acceptance tests every hour, and all the performance tests once a day. It's a game of confidence and this computer is here to help you feel better.

so, the system will be rebuilt and all of our tests will be run, using the latest code. Now that's automation!

Save the Logs

CruiseControl generates a log file every time it attempts a build. It's a good idea to save those files so that you can check on the build results later.

```
<log dir="logs/dms">
  <merge dir="checkout/dms/build/test-results" />
</log>
```

We'll use the logs directory created earlier as the dumping ground for log files. The dms subdirectory will be created to hold the dms project's log files. That is, the build log files are stored in a directory that isn't deleted every build cycle.

In addition to the log files that CruiseControl generates, you also want each build log to include the results of JUnit tests. Unfortunately, the test output is currently being displayed only on the console. You need to create a new `test` target that, when run, will also output the JUnit test results as XML files in the build/test-results directory of the project. This directory is used as the value of the `dir` attribute of the *<merge>* element. CruiseControl will then merge the contents of that directory into the build log.

Generate Test Results As XML

When we ran our tests from the command line in the previous chapter, they output messages to the console. But when a scheduled build is run, nobody will be watching the console. We need to capture the test results in a format that can be displayed to us later in the CruiseControl build log.

Let's revisit the build.xml file and define a new build target that will run the tests and send the output to XML files.

```
<target name="test" depends="compile-tests">
  <delete dir="${test.xml.dir}"/>
  <mkdir dir="${test.xml.dir}"/>
  <junit errorProperty="test.failed"
         failureProperty="test.failed">
    <classpath refid="project.classpath" />
    <formatter type="brief" usefile="false" />
    <formatter type="xml" />
    <batchtest todir="${test.xml.dir}">
      <fileset dir="${build.test.dir}"
        includes="**/*Test.class" />
    </batchtest>
    <sysproperty key="doc.dir" value="${doc.dir}" />
    <sysproperty key="index.dir" value="${index.dir}" />
  </junit>
  <fail message="Tests failed! Check test reports."
    if="test.failed" />
</target>
```

This `test` target is similar to the `test` target from the last chapter, but has a few important differences. First, it always creates an empty directory to hold the JUnit test results.

```
<delete dir="${test.xml.dir}"/>
<mkdir dir="${test.xml.dir}"/>
```

The `test.xml.dir` property, defined in the properties section of the build.xml file, points to the project's build/test-results directory. This is the directory that CruiseControl uses as the source for merging test results into the build log.

Instead of halting on the first test failure, the *<junit>* task sets a `test.failed` property on either an error or a failure.

```
<junit errorProperty="test.failed"
       failureProperty="test.failed">
```

This makes sure that all the tests results—successes and failures—are collected in XML files. Notice that later in the file we use the `test.failed` property in the *<fail>* task to alert us if one or more tests failed.

To output test results to the console and to XML files, define both a `brief` and an `xml` formatter.

```
<formatter type="brief" usefile="false" />
<formatter type="xml" />
```

The *<batchtest>* task needs to be changed to include a `todir` attribute. This attribute defines the output directory for the XML files generated by the XML formatter.

```
<batchtest todir="${test.xml.dir}">
  <fileset dir="${build.test.dir}"
    includes="**/*Test.class" />
</batchtest>
```

Now we have a new `test` target that generates XML files, in addition to showing test results on the console. CruiseControl will use those XML files when it generates a build log. This feature will come in handy later when we send the build status to the team.

Publish Build Results

publishers

Finally, back in the config.xml file, you need to specify *publishers*—things to be notified after the build cycle happens.

```
<publishers>
  <currentbuildstatuspublisher
    file="logs/dms/currentbuildstatus.txt" />
</publishers>
```

```
<cruisecontrol>
  <project name="dms" buildafterfailed="false">

    <bootstrappers>
      <currentbuildstatusbootstrapper
        file="logs/dms/currentbuildstatus.txt" />
    </bootstrappers>
    <modificationset quietperiod="60">
      <cvs localworkingcopy="checkout/dms" />
    </modificationset>
    <schedule interval="60">
      <ant buildfile="cc-build.xml" target="build" />
    </schedule>
    <log dir="logs/dms">
      <merge dir="checkout/dms/build/test-results" />
    </log>
    <publishers>
      <currentbuildstatuspublisher
        file="logs/dms/currentbuildstatus.txt" />
    </publishers>
  </project>
</cruisecontrol>
```

builds/config.xml

Figure 3.3: CRUISECONTROL CONFIGURATION FILE

The <currentbuildstatuspublisher> publisher simply writes a message to the logs/dms/currentbuildstatus.txt file indicating that the build cycle has finished. Similar to bootstrappers, the publishers are run regardless of whether a build was actually attempted. Think of this as CruiseControl punching out after a hard interval's work.

You've passed the test. You're now licensed to drive on Cruise-Control! Figure 3.3 shows the complete config.xml file.

OK, so that configuration exercise wasn't a leisurely Sunday drive, especially compared to the one-liner you wrote for cron. But from this point, you can easily get a lot more than cron offers. Moreover, now that you've configured CruiseControl for the first time, you can apply the same steps to put your other projects on a schedule.

3.3 Running CruiseControl

With the configuration file that tells CruiseControl everything it needs to know to run our build process in hand, we're ready to see some action! First, navigate to the builds directory that contains the config.xml and cc-build.xml files. Then run the CruiseControl script. On Unix, the commands are

```
$ cd ~/builds
$ $CC_HOME/main/bin/cruisecontrol.sh
```

Under Windows, the slashes swing around.

```
$ cd \builds
$ %CC_HOME%\main\bin\cruisecontrol.bat
```

CruiseControl will start up, read the config.xml file, and go right to work.

Starting Up

When CruiseControl starts up, the output can be verbose. It likes to let us know it's doing something useful as a result of our configuration effort. Here's the important information:

```
projectName = [dms]
Project dms:  reading settings from config file
              [/Users/mike/builds/config.xml]
Project dms starting
Project dms:  next build in 1 minutes
Project dms:  idle
```

If the output you see doesn't look so hopeful, then perhaps you need to tweak your config.xml file. Thankfully, you don't have to restart CruiseControl to change the configuration. It will reload the config.xml file every time a build cycle starts. You can make any necessary changes and simply wait another minute for it to notice.

Then You Wait...

Now wait patiently as 60 long seconds go by. CruiseControl then wakes up on schedule to check if there's any work.

```
Project dms:  in build queue
Project dms:  reading settings from config file
              [/Users/mike/builds/config.xml]
Project dms:  bootstrapping
Project dms:  checking for modifications
Project dms:  2 modifications have been detected.
Project dms:  now building
```

When it wakes up, it first reloads the config.xml file. Then it checks the CVS repository and finds that something has been modified. This being the first build cycle, CruiseControl may or may not detect changes in your repository. It needs to establish a baseline and you may have to change a file in your repository to force CruiseControl to run a build. Assuming it detects a change, it's ready to run the build.

...Until a Build Is Attempted

This is where you finally get to experience the fruits of your labors. At long last, you will see the one-step build process get run automatically by the computer.

```
Buildfile: cc-build.xml
build:
[delete] Deleting directory /Users/mike/builds/checkout/dms
[cvs] Using cvs passfile: /Users/mike/.cvspass
[cvs] U dms/README
[cvs] U dms/build.xml
...
prepare:
[mkdir] Created dir: /Users/mike/builds/checkout/dms/build/prod
[mkdir] Created dir: /Users/mike/builds/checkout/dms/build/test
compile:
[javac] Compiling 4 source files to /Users/.../dms/build/prod
compile-tests:
[javac] Compiling 3 source files to /Users/.../dms/build/test
test:
[junit] Testsuite: com.pragprog.dms.SearchTest
...
BUILD SUCCESSFUL
```

A lot happened here. The build target of the cc-build.xml file ran. It deleted the checkout/dms directory and then re-created it by checking out the dms project from CVS.

Then the test target of the build.xml file ran. That Ant target has dependencies on other targets, such as the compile target. As you'd expect, all the dependent targets are run prior to running the tests. And miracle of miracles, the project built successfully!

Having run the build, CruiseControl records the results in a log file, notifies the publishers that indeed it showed up for work on time, and then promptly goes back to sleep.

```
Project dms:  merging accumulated log files
Project dms:  publishing build results
Project dms:  idle
Project dms:  next build in 1 minutes
```

Once CruiseControl is started, it keeps running regardless of whether the last build succeeded or failed. It awakens on cue to check if a build is necessary, and if so goes about the

Joe Asks...

What About Anthill?

Another build scheduler that's definitely worth exploring is Anthill.* It's available in either an open-source version (Anthill OS) or, for those who need some chrome under the hood, there's Anthill Pro.

Opinions vary as to whether CruiseControl or Anthill is easier to install and configure. It really depends on what you consider easy. To run Anthill you deploy a WAR file into your favorite servlet engine and then configure it through a web interface. CruiseControl, on the other hand, can be configured and run via the command line without ever firing up a servlet engine. It's easier to demonstrate scheduled builds using CruiseControl as it doesn't require a servlet engine.

Remember, the choice of a tool isn't as important as getting your build scheduled as soon as possible. So use whatever tool helps you do that.

---

*http://www.urbancode.com/projects/anthill

business of attempting a build. Then it goes to sleep until the next build interval. Rinse and repeat. It's a pretty dull life, which is exactly why we're happy not to be doing it ourselves.

Now It's Your Turn

CruiseControl is now in its rhythmic build loop waiting for us to do what we're paid to do. Every minute it wakes up, notices that we haven't touched anything in CVS, and goes back to sleep.

```
Project dms:  No modifications found, build not necessary.
Project dms:  idle
Project dms:  next build in 1 minutes
```

And it's happy to just keep doing this and enjoying a life of leisure. But we're not going to stand for that kind of lackadaisical behavior—we want to see if it's really watching the CVS repository and not asleep at the switch.

In the ~/work directory, there is a checked-out local copy of the dms project. Now we'll change a Java source file. But suppose in our haste we unknowingly introduce a bug. Worse yet, we forget to run our unit tests before checking in the modified source file.

```
$ cd ~/work/dms
$ emacs src/com/pragprog/dms/Search.java
(Hack, hack, hack)
$ cvs commit -m "I'm too busy to test"
```

Now we wait around for the build timer to pop. When it does, CruiseControl checks for work. Again, the output is verbose, but it vaguely resembles the following:

```
1 modification has been detected.
Project dms:  now building

Buildfile: cc-build.xml

build:
[delete] Deleting directory /Users/mike/builds/checkout/dms
[cvs] Using cvs passfile: /Users/mike/.cvspass
[cvs] U dms/README
[cvs] U dms/build.xml
...
prepare:
...
compile:
...
compile-tests:
...
test:
[junit] Testsuite: com.pragprog.dms.SearchTest
[junit] Tests run: 2, Failures: 1, Errors: 0, Time elapsed: 1.957 sec

[junit] Testcase: testTitleSearch(com.pragprog.dms.SearchTest): FAILED
[junit] expected:[2]  but was:[0]
...
BUILD FAILED
```

Uh oh! We just got busted. CruiseControl can't do much for us other than record the failure in the log file and tell us to fix things before the next build interval. Rest assured, we won't have to spend our days monitoring the build machine. We'll automate the notification of a build failure through email a bit later and explore advanced monitoring techniques in Section 6.1, *Monitoring Scheduled Builds*, on page 127.

What a Scheduled Build Is Good For

We got sloppy. It happens to the best of us from time to time, so we need somebody looking over our shoulder. In this case, that somebody is CruiseControl. It noticed that a modification was made to the CVS repository, and it attempted to run the tests against those changes. But the test is expecting one value and got another, so it fails. It's not the ideal situation, but at least you now know there's a problem and you can fix it before it turns into a costly problem later.

Now before you do anything else short of breathing, you need to get the build back to a steady state. Make the necessary changes to the local copy of the project in the ~/work/dms directory. And run the tests before checking in this time! Then sit back and wait for the next build interval.

A minute later CruiseControl builds the project and confirms that indeed you're still the world's greatest programmer. Better yet, it will continue watching for changes and running all the tests while you're off doing what you're good at—writing programs.

3.4 Publishing the Build Status

The build is now running on a schedule, but you're missing something important. Unless a real, live human watches the console output of CruiseControl, you won't know when the build breaks.

When a build fails, we'd like something to send up a flare, sound the alarm, and start brewing a fresh pot of coffee. Failing all that, an email will do.

Sending Build Results via Email

We have a lot of options when it comes to who gets what kind of email, but let's keep it simple. We're interested only in getting an email when the build fails and when it has been fixed. And once we get an email that tells us the build has failed, we don't care to continue getting more email until we're back on stable ground. Less is more in this case. If we're constantly being bombarded with build email, we'll stop reading them. It's like signing up for a newsgroup. All the posts are interesting...for the first day.

Notification by email is relatively easy with CruiseControl.[4] Just add an email publisher.

---

[4]See [HL02] for details on how to send a build failure email using Ant.

```
<htmlemail mailhost="your.smtp.host"
  returnaddress="cruisecontrol@clarkware.com"
  defaultsuffix="@clarkware.com"
  buildresultsurl="http://localhost:8080/cruisecontrol/buildresults/dms"
  css="/Users/mike/tools/cruisecontrol/reporting/jsp/css/cruisecontrol.css"
  xsldir="/Users/mike/tools/cruisecontrol/reporting/jsp/xsl"
  logdir="logs/dms">

  <map alias="manager" address="bigcheese@clarkware.com" />
  <map alias="mike" address="mike@clarkware.com" />
  <map alias="fred" address="fred@somewhere.com" />

  <always address="manager" />
  <failure address="mike" reportWhenFixed="true" />
  <failure address="fred" reportWhenFixed="true" />
</htmlemail>
```

Add this *<htmlemail>* element inside the *<publishers>* element of config.xml. Even though the build is failing, we'd like the email to be nicely formatted HTML. Figure 3.4 on the next page shows what arrives in our inbox. Notice that it includes test failure details because we merged our JUnit test results into the CruiseControl log. It also lists all the modifications that were made—and who made those modifications!—since the last successful build. Perhaps you know where the guilty party lives.

In the interest of sanity, we're going to gloss over the details of email configuration here. Most of it is self-explanatory. However, there are a few things worth noting, starting from the top:

```
<htmlemail mailhost="your.smtp.host"
  returnaddress="cruisecontrol@clarkware.com"
  defaultsuffix="@clarkware.com"
  buildresultsurl="http://localhost:8080/cruisecontrol/buildresults/dms"
  css="/Users/mike/tools/cruisecontrol/reporting/jsp/css/cruisecontrol.css"
  xsldir="/Users/mike/tools/cruisecontrol/reporting/jsp/xsl"
  logdir="logs/dms">
```

The `logdir` directory points to the directory CruiseControl uses for saving each build log. To format the email, it applies a style through the formatting wonders of the `css` and `xsldir` attributes to the latest build log. If you don't particularly like the default email format, you have the power of CSS and XSLT at your fingertips.

Next, create email aliases for each user that should receive an email.

```
<map alias="manager" address="bigcheese@clarkware.com" />
<map alias="mike" address="mike@clarkware.com" />
<map alias="fred" address="fred@somewhere.com" />
```

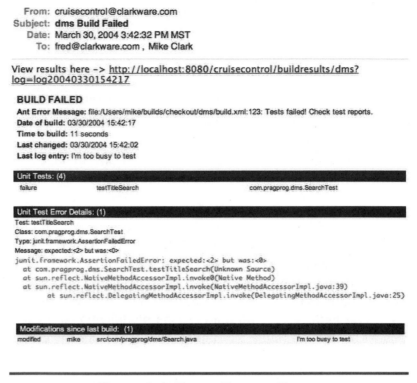

From: cruisecontrol@clarkware.com
Subject: **dms Build Failed**
Date: March 30, 2004 3:42:32 PM MST
To: fred@clarkware.com , Mike Clark

View results here -> http://localhost:8080/cruisecontrol/buildresults/dms?
log=log20040330154217

BUILD FAILED

Ant Error Message: file:/Users/mike/builds/checkout/dms/build.xml:123: Tests failed! Check test reports.

Date of build: 03/30/2004 15:42:17

Time to build: 11 seconds

Last changed: 03/30/2004 15:42:02

Last log entry: I'm too busy to test

Unit Tests: (4)

failure	testTitleSearch	com.pragprog.dms.SearchTest

Unit Test Error Details: (1)

Test: testTitleSearch
Class: com.pragprog.dms.SearchTest
Type: junit.framework.AssertionFailedError
Message: expected:<2> but was:<0>

```
junit.framework.AssertionFailedError: expected:<2> but was:<0>
    at com.pragprog.dms.SearchTest.testTitleSearch(Unknown Source)
    at sun.reflect.NativeMethodAccessorImpl.invoke0(Native Method)
    at sun.reflect.NativeMethodAccessorImpl.invoke(NativeMethodAccessorImpl.java:39)
        at sun.reflect.DelegatingMethodAccessorImpl.invoke(DelegatingMethodAccessorImpl.java:25)
```

Modifications since last build: (1)

modified	mike	src/com/pragprog/dms/Search.java	I'm too busy to test

Figure 3.4: BUILD FAILURE EMAIL

Using the <map> element, each member of our team is associated with their corresponding email address. Without any mappings in place, CruiseControl will use the CVS username and the value of the defaultsuffix attribute. In this example, it's not necessary to map "mike" to "mike@clarkware.com" if "mike" is a CVS user. That's taken care of when the email publisher applies the value of the defaultsuffix attribute. Our manager needs to have an email address mapped because he wants email, but he's not a CVS user. And Fred wants his email sent to an address different from that in the default-suffix attribute, so we have to define a specific mapping for him.

By default, CruiseControl sends email on a success or a failure to those folks who checked stuff in since the last successful build. We can get a bit more control by defining exactly what kind of email each mapped user receives.

```
<always address="manager" />
<failure address="mike" reportWhenFixed="true" />
<failure address="fred" reportWhenFixed="true" />
```

Using the <*always*> element, we make sure our manager gets an email for both successful and failed builds. That just happens to be his preference. He doesn't make changes to CVS, so we need to explicitly declare him as an email recipient.

All the programmers should know when the software *isn't* building. As a team, *we* need to get it fixed pronto. (Oh, and a little peer pressure goes a long way on some teams.) Use the <*failure*> element to list programmers as recipients of email when the build fails. It's also important for the programmers to know when the build is fixed, so set the value of the reportWhenFixed attribute to true to get those emails as rewards for fixing the build. You may want to set up an alias in your email system for all the developers on your team and send an email to that alias when the build fails and when it's fixed.

You may have noticed that the build status email includes a "View results here" hyperlink at the top. Let's see what that's all about.

Pulling Build History from a Web Page

It's nice to have the build status forwarded via email. But when it comes time to debug build failures, it's also convenient to have a historical record of all the builds. When you need that information, you can pull it from a web page.

The standard CruiseControl distribution includes an optional web reporting project in the $CC_HOME/reporting/jsp directory. Building this project creates a WAR file that can be dropped into your favorite servlet engine, such as Tomcat.

Build and Deploy the Web Application

First, you need to define three properties that tell the web application where to find files and directories in your build workspace. In the $CC_HOME/reporting/jsp directory, create a file called override.properties that defines the following properties (substitute your absolute builds directory):

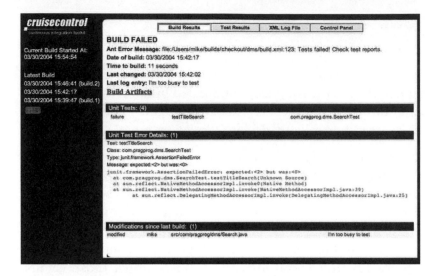

Figure 3.5: BUILD HISTORY WEB PAGE

```
user.log.dir=/Users/mike/builds/logs
user.build.status.file=currentbuildstatus.txt
cruise.build.artifacts.dir=/Users/mike/builds/logs
```

Next, build the web application. On Unix type the following:

```
$ cd $CC_HOME/reporting/jsp
$ sh build.sh war
```

This incantation creates a cruisecontrol.war file in the directory $CC_HOME/reporting/jsp/dist. Deploy this WAR file into your server. If you're using Tomcat on Unix, for example, type

```
$ cp dist/cruisecontrol.war $TOMCAT_HOME/webapps
```

View the Build History

With your server running and the CruiseControl web application deployed, click the hyperlink at the top of a build results email or browse to

```
http://buildmachine:port/cruisecontrol/buildresults/dms
```

This will take you to a web page similar to the one shown in Figure 3.5.

Along the left side of this page is a list of all the builds that were attempted. Clicking any build shows the details you see in the right area. This is the same information you'll see in emails sent by the <*htmlemail*> publisher.

Now you have build results being pushed via email, and anybody with access to the web server can actively pull a detailed history of builds from a web page. That's a good start, but in Section 6.1, *Monitoring Scheduled Builds*, on page 127 we'll explore how to get feedback about builds in other cool and exciting ways.

3.5 Scaling Up

If while reading this chapter you've been wondering if Cruise-Control can handle all the code in your Java project, then wonder no longer. Here's a glimpse of CruiseControl on a massive, real-world project:

CruiseControl on a Large Scale
by Jared Richardson, Software Manager, SAS Institute

Many people think that open-source projects can't scale to the enterprise level, but CruiseControl is an example of one that does. This is our success story of how flexible and extensible CruiseControl is.

We have approximately 800 developers working on more than 250 projects with five million lines of Java code. Some of these projects are very low-level components, some are portlets, and some are end-user solutions. We were able to get all five million lines of Java code under continuous integration using CruiseControl relatively easily. In fact, as I type this, we are covering three code branches, so we are really covering 15 million lines of code, and the CruiseControl box is a single CPU x86 machine.

We used a few tricks to get CruiseControl running at the enterprise level. First, we multithreaded CruiseControl ourselves. (Those changes should be in the next release of CC.) This is one of the advantages of working with an open-source project!

Next, instead of using the regular CVS modification set, we are using the *compound modification set*. It contains a *trigger* that initiates the build and a *target* that is used to actually get the file changes. For our trigger, we use the filesystem modification set. When a project changes in CVS, a CVS trigger touches a single file that CruiseControl is monitoring. This prevents CruiseControl from trying to poll CVS every ten minutes for changes in 15 million lines of code. Once it sees that a project trigger file has changed, it uses the regular CVS modification set—the target in the compound modification set—to see exactly what changes were made.

Will Gwaltney, another SAS employee, wrote the compound modification set, and we contributed it back to the CruiseControl project. Now anyone can use a compound modification set, and you can use any of the CruiseControl modification sets as either triggers or targets.

We use one trick that isn't stock. We have a build grid at SAS that has a number of machines behind it. We are able to ask it to do the builds for us, and it finds an available machine. This keeps the load of building the systems off the CruiseControl box.

All in all, CC was very easy to roll out and is now part of the standard Java development experience at SAS. With very little effort, you can get this same type of coverage at your company, no matter the size of the code base.

That's right, Jared, no project is too big to be built on a schedule! Indeed, the more code you have, the more you need continuous integration to keep it in check. After all, would you want to be running builds of that proportion manually to get confidence that it's always working? You might have to use a few clever tricks, but it's well worth it in the end. And with CruiseControl, you already have a powerful scheduler that's free. Of course, this is just the beginning of what CruiseControl can do. To learn more, visit the CruiseControl wiki.[5]

What We Just Did

We've come a long way in this chapter. We started with a one-step build process that we previously ran manually from the command line. Then we scheduled that command to run at regular intervals so that the project is continually integrated

---

[5]http://confluence.public.thoughtworks.org/display/CC/Home

and tested. We can even schedule multiple Ant targets, each running on a different schedule. The build scheduler alerts us when the build breaks by sending email and recording the build history on a common web page. All this makes finding and fixing problems easier so that we have more time to do the really exciting stuff.

Chapter 4

Push-Button Releases

All this fuss about building and testing software is important, but it's just a means to an end. After all, you get paid to deliver working software of value to customers. Everything up to this point is just resumé building unless you can easily generate a release, and consistently regenerate it, to capitalize on your development efforts. You can't stop at just automating the build and test cycle.

In this chapter we'll focus on the bottom line: generating a release of software. Automating the release procedure sets us up to release new versions of our software, or regenerate any prior release, at the push of a button.

4.1 Releasing Early and Often

As it stands, the *DMS* project is still rather trivial. The build process compiles a few Java files and runs unit tests in a matter of seconds. We're successfully creating builds locally by manually running the Ant build file and automatically on the machine that runs scheduled builds. Before things get any more complicated, however, we need to start generating releases of our software.

The Contents of a Release

A *software release* is a packaged collection of files intended for some customer of our software. The exact contents of a release may vary, but most software releases consist of at least the following:

software release

- A release is uniquely identified by a name and a version number. The name typically bears some resemblance to the name of the software product as defined by marketing. The version number is generally a combination of a major and minor version number. For example, a bug-fix release of the second version of our *DMS* project might be identified as the dms-2.1 release.

- Each release is defined by the set of features it includes. That is, we generate a release when we've built features that offer value to the end user. That might mean we wait for a dozen features to be developed or for a single bug to be fixed.

- Each release is complete. All the files necessary to run all the features of the software are included. All the documentation related to that release is also included. Users like us more when this happens.

- If installing a release requires following a set of instructions, those instructions are carried out by running a single installation script or utility.

Whether we're generating a release for our project's QA team, the in-house project down the hall, or the entire computing world, we generate a release in the same consistent way.

4.2 Preparing for Your First Release

We've been heads-down on the *DMS* project for a week now implementing features for our first release. It's an exciting time, not because we're hoping to get rich selling this release, but because this is our first opportunity to actually release something. At the end of the day we'll be able to point to neatly packaged software and say, "We made that!" And as creators, that brings us great joy. It also gives the rest of our project team confidence in our ability to deliver.

Aiming Small

We'll be delivering this first release to the good folks on the QA team. That is, they'll serve as our internal customers. You can only do so much in a week, so the list of features that made it into this release is rather short. It's kind of difficult to generate a release now, while the project is small and the build process is fast—and it will only get more difficult as the project continues. So we should start generating releases before the job gets any bigger. If we aim small, we can only miss small.

Synchronizing Work for the Release

All week the programmers have been hard at work on new features: checking files out of version control, making changes, running tests, and checking the files back in. Meanwhile, the scheduled build is running on a frequent interval to keep all the code integrated.

At the end of the week, everybody working on the release needs to synchronize their local workspace with the shared repository. They make sure all their tests pass, then type

```
$ cd ~/work/dms
$ cvs commit -m "I'm done with this release"
cvs commit: Examining .
```

Sanity Checking the Work

At this point we take off our "programmer" hat and replace it with a "release manager" hat. (You might actually log in as a separate user for the remainder of this chapter.)

Despite the good intentions of programmers, it's not uncommon for them to forget to check in a local file. Perhaps a local file was never added to the repository, so running the cvs commit command ignores it. When this happens, a "Works on my machine" debugging session soon follows. The scheduled build process will notify us when files are missing, but we can conserve our release-manager hairline slightly by running a quick sanity check before going any further.

Let's make sure we can build and test the code we're about to copy into the release branch. First, check out a fresh copy of the files currently in the version control repository into a nondevelopment directory.

```
$ rm -r ~/work/dms
$ cd ~/work
$ cvs co dms
```

Then run the `test` target of the build file.

```
$ cd ~/work/dms
$ ant test
Buildfile: build.xml
...
BUILD SUCCESSFUL
```

Seeing that neon BUILD SUCCESSFUL sign gives us confidence to proceed to the next step.

Creating a Release Branch

At this point the mainline of the version control repository contains the master copy of all the files we'll put into the release. There's just one problem: At the same time that we're preparing the release, someone could change a file on the mainline. If that were to happen, the contents of our release may become inconsistent.

We could lock the version control repository until we've successfully generated the release, but in effect that blocks everyone from starting on the next release. Alternatively, we could create a copy of all the files that will go into the release into a temporary directory. But then let's assume you fix a bug or need to make a minor enhancement to a file while preparing the release. How do you also make those changes to the master copy under version control? And after you've delivered the release to QA and deleted the temporary directory, how do you regenerate the release to fix bugs QA might find?

A much more reliable option is to use the version control repository to create a stable working area for the release. After all, it's designed to keep track of file changes so you can recover any version of a file at any time. By creating what's *release branch* commonly called a *release branch* in the repository, you can isolate yourself from activity on the live mainline while preparing this release.

Now that we know the mainline of the repository contains everything for the release, we're ready to create the release branch. To do that, run the cvs rtag command.

```
$ cd ~/work/dms
$ cvs rtag -b RB_1_0 dms
```

You can run the cvs rtag command from anywhere because it ignores what's in the local directory. Instead, it takes a snap-

---

☺ Joe Asks...

Can I Do This with My Version Control System?

In this chapter we're focused on releasing software with consistency and repeatability. A version control system is merely a tool that helps us do that. It keeps track of file versions, creates multiple copies of those versioned files in separate branches, and applies named tags to a set of versioned files.

Branching and tagging are concepts supported by most version control systems. That is, while the syntax for how to create branches and tags differs across version control systems, the concepts are universal. And frankly, if your version control system doesn't support the basic concepts demonstrated in this chapter, then trade it in for one that does.

Although the examples in this chapter use CVS, it's not the only version control system in the known universe. If you're using another version control system on your project, then feel free to gloss over the CVS syntax. If you aren't yet using a version control system, or you aren't familiar with branching and tagging in CVS, please see (TH03).

---

shot of the files in the version control system's repository. The -b option creates a branch off of the mainline that contains a copy of all the files in the dms module. It also tags all of those files with the RB_1_0 branch tag.

Now you have a release branch named RB_1_0 for version 1.0 of the *DMS* project. Think of the release branch as a copy of the files on the mainline at the time the branch was created. As compared to a temporary directory, a branch maintains its own history and the ability to efficiently merge changes back onto the mainline. After we've delivered the release, this branch will continue to be available. We can easily regenerate the release should we need to fix a bug reported by QA.

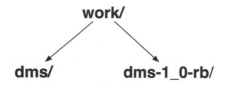

Figure 4.1: RELEASE BRANCH DIRECTORY

Checking Out the Release Branch

Creating the release branch had no effect on the local directory ~/work/dms. It's still working on the mainline. If you were to change a file in the local directory and check it in, the change would go onto the mainline, not the release branch.

To begin working on the release branch, you need to check it out. We'll name our branch's directory ~/work/dms-1_0-rb, which is parallel to our ~/work/dms directory. By appending the version number (1_0 in this case) to the release branch directory name, we'll know exactly which release version we're working on. Using an underscore between the major and minor version numbers keeps the name consistent with the convention used to name the release branch. By also appending rb to the directory name, we'll avoid confusing the release branch directory with the mainline directory.

To check out the release branch, specify the branch tag and override the default directory name.

```
$ cd ~/work
$ cvs co -r RB_1_0 -d dms-1_0-rb dms
cvs checkout: Updating dms-1_0-rb
U dms-1_0-rb/LICENSE
U dms-1_0-rb/README
U dms-1_0-rb/build.xml
...
```

The -r checkout option indicates the branch tag: RB_1_0. This checks out the most recent files in that branch. The -d checkout option overrides the default directory name so that the files are checked out under the ~/work/dms-1_0-rb directory. Figure 4.1 shows the two parallel directories we now have.

Testing the Release Branch

The first thing to do after checking out the release branch is test it. This is the same sanity check we made before creating the release branch. This time, instead of verifying that the mainline of the repository is up-to-date, we're verifying that those same files successfully made it into the release branch. Run the build in the release branch directory by typing

```
$ cd ~/work/dms-1.0-rb
$ ant test
Buildfile: build.xml
...
BUILD SUCCESSFUL
```

This step may seem a bit overcautious, but running all the tests is cheap insurance. Now you know that all the source files compile and the tests are passing. It stands to reason the release branch is intact, so we're confident in moving on to the next step.

Tweaking the Release Branch

At this point you have a release branch directory that contains files isolated from the repository's mainline. You can commit changes in this directory, and they'll be made to the release branch, and not the mainline. This allows you to make any necessary revisions to the files in preparation for the release.

Say, for example, you notice that the README file is missing a few minor details that will surely trip up QA when they get the release. To make those changes, edit the README file in the release branch directory and commit the change back.

```
$ cd ~/work/dms-1.0-rb
$ emacs README
$ cvs commit -m "Oops, forgot these important details!"
```

This updated version of the README file exists only on the release branch. To apply the same change to the mainline, you'd need to merge the file onto the mainline.

You can continue making edits in the release branch directory in preparation for generating the actual release. When you're done polishing, it's wise to run all the tests as a sanity check before moving on to the next step: packaging the release.

4.3 Packaging the Release

After the release branch directory has been polished, the code has compiled, and all the tests have run, we're in good shape. We now have a directory that contains source files, class files, vendor libraries, scripts, and even some documentation. Not too shabby for a first release. Indeed, this is an accomplishment to be proud of on any project. But it's not quite enough.

distribution file

The release needs to be in a package usable by a customer. So once we've built and tested the contents of the release branch directory, the next step in the release procedure calls for creating a *distribution file*. This is the file a customer would effectively pull off the shelf, take back to the office, and install with a minimum number of tools required.

Selecting Files for Distribution

When a customer unpacks the distribution file, presentation is everything. The way in which the files are organized and laid down on disk is a reflection of the software's quality. We want to put all the necessary parts and pieces into a neat little box that's clearly labeled so that its contents are obvious. And when the box is opened, the instructions should be right on top. That is, we want the distribution file to resemble a software *product* rather than a development *project*.

The first step toward packaging the release is to carefully select which files from our release branch directory will go into the distribution file. Figure 4.2 on the next page shows the transformation process from the release branch directory to the directory structure in the distribution file. When the customer unpacks the distribution file, we want them to get the directory structure on the right.

Notice that not everything makes the cut—only a subset of the files in the directory on the left make it into the distribution directory on the right. If you think of this selection process as being like a playground game of dodgeball, here's who *doesn't* get picked to play for the distribution team:

- *Development tools.* Customers won't be building the software, so they don't need development tools. For example, the build.xml file is not distributed. Also, any vendor

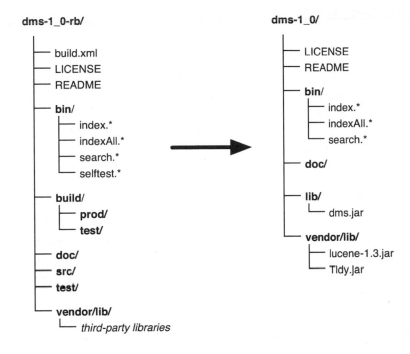

```
dms-1_0-rb/                          dms-1_0/

├── build.xml                        ├── LICENSE
├── LICENSE                          ├── README
├── README                          
│                                    ├── bin/
├── bin/                             │   ├── index.*
│   ├── index.*                      │   ├── indexAll.*
│   ├── indexAll.*                   │   └── search.*
│   ├── search.*                    
│   └── selftest.*                   ├── doc/
│                                   
├── build/                           ├── lib/
│   ├── prod/                        │   └── dms.jar
│   └── test/                       
│                                    └── vendor/lib/
├── doc/                                 ├── lucene-1.3.jar
├── src/                                 └── Tidy.Jar
├── test/                           
│                                   
└── vendor/lib/                     
    └── third-party libraries       
```

Figure 4.2: STANDARD DISTRIBUTION FILE CONTENTS

---

libraries that are needed only for building (not running) our software, such as junit-3.8.jar, don't make the team.

- *Build inputs.* Unless this is an open-source project, customers don't need, nor do we want to give them, any of the inputs to the build process. The src and test directories, for example, aren't included in the distribution file.

- *Test classes.* We won't be distributing our tests as part of the standard distribution. So the build/test directory stays behind for now. This is another reason to keep all the test classes in their own directory—it helps avoid accidentally distributing them.

- *Individual production class files.* The production classes in the build/prod directory on the left do get picked, but in a different form. They are first bundled into the lib/dms.jar file on the right. This means we can easily replace all the class files by distributing an updated dms.jar file later.

Packing the Distribution File

Once you've determined the contents of the distribution file, you're ready to do the actual packing, putting your files into a nice tidy box. But what kind of box? There are many options, but the *ZIP* and *tar* varieties are most popular. Pick the appropriate type for your customers. We'll put our release in a ZIP file. If you prefer to distribute tar files, then it's simply a word substitution from here on.

Write a Packaging Script

When it comes to writing the script that packs the distribution file, we're faced with another decision. We'll need something that runs the jar command to bundle our class files into a JAR file and then runs the zip command to create a distribution file containing all the necessary files.

We could use a shell script or a batch file. However, Ant has a *<jar>* and a *<zip>* task that both offer conveniences over the command-line versions. Since we're already familiar with Ant's syntax, let's drop back into Ant for this step.

Start by creating an Ant build file called package.xml. The complete file is shown in Figure 4.3 on page 86. The first line defines a project.

```
<project name="dms" default="zip" basedir=".">
```

This project has a default target called zip that creates the distribution ZIP file.

Define Packaging Properties

After defining the project, add three properties to define the release by its unique name and version number.

```
<property name="name"    value="dms" />
<property name="version" value="x.y" />
<property name="release" value="${name}-${version}" />
```

Using properties to define the release is convenient because it means you can override these properties when invoking Ant from the command line. For example, let's say you run the package.xml file like so:

```
$ ant -buildfile package.xml -Dversion=1.0
```

When Ant runs the package.xml file with the -Dversion=1.0 option, the value of the release property used during packaging will be dms-1.0. This means you don't have to change the Ant build file when you update to new release versions.

Next, use properties to define the location of the production class files and the directory that will ultimately contain the distribution file.

```
<property name="build.prod.dir" location="build/prod"/>
<property name="dist.dir"       location="dist" />
```

Following those properties, define four additional properties that refer to the JAR and ZIP files.

```
<property name="jar.name" value="${name}.jar" />
<property name="jar.path" location="${dist.dir}/${jar.name}" />
<property name="zip.name" value="${release}.zip" />
<property name="zip.path" location="${dist.dir}/${zip.name}" />
```

Notice how these properties use the release name and version to name the JAR and ZIP files. The JAR file's name will include the project name, so it will be called dms.jar. The ZIP file's name will include the project name *and* the version number, as defined by the release property. For example, the first release will be packaged in a ZIP file called dms-1.0.zip. Notice that both of these files will be created in the directory pointed to by the dist.dir property (dist in this case).

The targets we'll write next will use these properties rather than the actual filenames. Defining the filenames and locations as properties makes it easy to change the naming convention later, if necessary. This also allows you to override the filenames from the command line.

Create a JAR File

The first target of package.xml file creates a JAR file containing all the production class files.

```
<target name="jar">
  <mkdir dir="${dist.dir}"/>
  <jar destfile="${jar.path}" basedir="${build.prod.dir}" />
</target>
```

The jar target first creates the distribution directory. It then uses the <jar> task to package all the classes in the build/prod directory into the resulting dist/dms.jar file.

Create a ZIP File

The second target of the package.xml file creates a ZIP file containing all the files in the distribution.

```
<target name="zip" depends="jar">
  <zip destfile="${zip.path}">
    <zipfileset dir="${basedir}" prefix="${release}">
      <include name="README" />
      <include name="LICENSE" />
    </zipfileset>
    <zipfileset dir="bin" filemode="755" prefix="${release}/bin">
      <include name="index.*" />
      <include name="indexAll.*" />
      <include name="search.*" />
    </zipfileset>
    <zipfileset dir="doc"  prefix="${release}/doc" />
    <zipfileset dir="dist" includes="${jar.name}"
                        prefix="${release}/lib" />
    <zipfileset dir="vendor" prefix="${release}/vendor">
      <include name="**/lucene-1.3.jar" />
      <include name="**/Tidy.jar" />
    </zipfileset>
  </zip>
</target>
```

Ant will ensure that the jar target is run to generate the JAR file before the zip target because of the declared dependency. The zip target then uses the <zip> task to copy specific files in the release branch directory into a ZIP file.

By using <zipfileset> elements you can control exactly which files get packaged into the distribution ZIP file and where those files are placed. This means you can organize the distribution file for the best presentation to your customers. For example:

- Only specific scripts from the bin directory are included in the bin directory of the ZIP file. Setting the filemode of the scripts to 0755 ensures that everyone is permitted to read and execute the scripts, but only the file owner has write permission.

- The dms.jar file was created in the dist directory by the jar target. In this step it's copied into the lib directory of the ZIP file.

- Only two vendor libraries are included from the vendor/lib directory—that's all that's needed to run the software.

- All the files and directories in the ZIP file are organized under a parent directory named for our release, as specified by using the prefix attribute on all the <zipfileset> elements. This means that when the customer unzips the distribution file for version 1.0, all its files will be under the dms-1.0 directory.

Now you have a script that automates the packing step. With it, you can create an infinite number of distribution files. Figure 4.3 on the next page shows the contents of the final package.xml file. Running this script with a specific version number creates a ZIP file whose structure mirrors that shown on the right side of Figure 4.2 on page 81.

Packing an Optional Test Distribution File

When we created the distribution file, it didn't contain any test classes. Normally, we don't want to ship our tests as part of the standard distribution because it might make the distribution file unreasonably large.

However, if a customer experiences a problem with our software once it's been installed, we'd like to know what went wrong. In that case, it would be beneficial to provide an optional distribution file that includes the tests and a push-button script to run them. Then we could ask the customer to install this optional distribution file, run the tests, and send us the results for analysis.

While we're in the packaging mode, it's easy to use all the same Ant tricks we just learned to create an optional distribution file for testing purposes. Figure 4.4 on page 87 shows the transformation process from the release branch directory to the directory structure in the optional test distribution file.

When a customer unpacks the test distribution file, they'll get the directory structure on the right. By unpacking this file in the same directory that contains our dms-1.0 installation, they'll be adding another layer of support to the standard installation. That is, they'll have a standard distribution that *also* includes everything needed to run diagnostic tests.

The package-tests.xml script shown in Figure 4.5 on page 88 is very similar to the package.xml script we just wrote. In

```xml
<?xml version="1.0"?>
<project name="dms" default="zip" basedir=".">
  <property name="name"      value="dms" />
  <property name="version" value="x_y" />
  <property name="release" value="${name}-${version}" />

  <property name="build.prod.dir" location="build/prod"/>
  <property name="dist.dir"       location="dist" />

  <property name="jar.name" value="${name}.jar" />
  <property name="jar.path" location="${dist.dir}/${jar.name}" />
  <property name="zip.name" value="${release}.zip" />
  <property name="zip.path" location="${dist.dir}/${zip.name}" />

  <target name="jar">
    <mkdir dir="${dist.dir}"/>
    <jar destfile="${jar.path}" basedir="${build.prod.dir}" />
  </target>

  <target name="zip" depends="jar">

    <zip destfile="${zip.path}">
      <zipfileset dir="${basedir}" prefix="${release}">
        <include name="README" />
        <include name="LICENSE" />
      </zipfileset>
      <zipfileset dir="bin" filemode="755" prefix="${release}/bin">
        <include name="index.*" />
        <include name="indexAll.*" />
        <include name="search.*" />
      </zipfileset>
      <zipfileset dir="doc"  prefix="${release}/doc" />
      <zipfileset dir="dist" includes="${jar.name}"
                             prefix="${release}/lib" />
      <zipfileset dir="vendor" prefix="${release}/vendor">
        <include name="**/lucene-1.3.jar" />
        <include name="**/Tidy.jar" />
      </zipfileset>
    </zip>

  </target>
</project>
```

dms/package.xml

Figure 4.3: STANDARD DISTRIBUTION PACKAGING SCRIPT

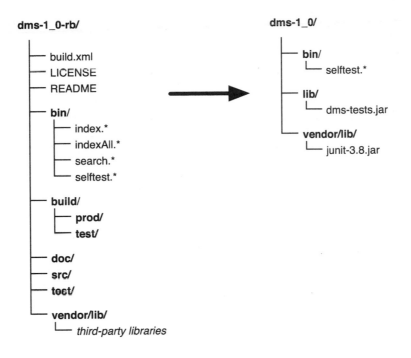

```
dms-1_0-rb/
     ├── build.xml
     ├── LICENSE
     ├── README
     │
     ├── bin/
     │    ├── index.*
     │    ├── indexAll.*
     │    ├── search.*
     │    └── selftest.*
     │
     ├── build/
     │    ├── prod/
     │    └── test/
     │
     ├── doc/
     ├── src/
     ├── toct/
     │
     └── vendor/lib/
          └── third-party libraries


dms-1_0/
     ├── bin/
     │    └── selftest.*
     │
     ├── lib/
     │    └── dms-tests.jar
     │
     └── vendor/lib/
          └── junit-3.8.jar
```

Figure 4.4: TEST DISTRIBUTION FILE CONTENTS

this case, however, the targets create dms-tests.jar, a JAR file containing just the test classes, and dms-1_0-tests.zip, a ZIP file containing the dms-tests.jar file and all additional files needed to run the tests.

We'll put this test distribution file to good use when we discuss how our customers install the software in Section 5.4, *Troubleshooting with Diagnostic Tests*, on page 103. The point to remember is that you can create multiple distribution files each with a subset of the files in the project directory. Then you can unpack them individually to layer on additional support to the standard distribution.

4.4 Generating the Release

Everything up to this point has been preparation. Preparation is key, but now it's time to actually generate the release.

```xml
<?xml version="1.0"?>
<project name="dms-tests" default="zip" basedir=".">
  <property name="name"          value="dms" />
  <property name="version"       value="x.y" />
  <property name="release"       value="${name}-${version}" />

  <property name="build.test.dir" location="build/test"/>
  <property name="dist.dir"       location="dist" />

  <property name="jar.name" value="${name}-tests.jar" />
  <property name="jar.path" location="${dist.dir}/${jar.name}" />
  <property name="zip.name" value="${release}-tests.zip" />
  <property name="zip.path" location="${dist.dir}/${zip.name}" />

  <target name="jar">
    <mkdir dir="${dist.dir}"/>
    <jar destfile="${jar.path}" basedir="${build.test.dir}" />
  </target>

  <target name="zip" depends="jar">

    <zip destfile="${zip.path}">
      <zipfileset dir="bin" filemode="755" prefix="${release}/bin">
        <include name="selftest.*" />
      </zipfileset>
      <zipfileset dir="dist" includes="${jar.name}"
        prefix="${release}/lib" />
      <zipfileset dir="vendor" prefix="${release}/vendor">
        <include name="**/junit-3.8.jar" />
      </zipfileset>
    </zip>
  </target>
</project>
```

dms/package-tests.xml

Figure 4.5: TEST DISTRIBUTION PACKAGING SCRIPT

Creating a Distribution File

Recall that earlier we tested the release branch. This involved
compiling the code and running the tests. This means all the
build outputs are ready for packaging. To create your first
distribution file, change back to the release branch directory
and run the package.xml script. Make sure to set the version
property with the appropriate version number.

```
$ cd ~/work/dms-1_0-rb
$ ant -buildfile package.xml -Dversion=1_0
Buildfile: package.xml

jar:
[mkdir] Created dir: /Users/mike/work/dms-1_0-rb/dist
[jar] Building jar: /Users/mike/work/dms-1_0-rb/dist/dms.jar
zip:
```

```
[zip] Building zip: /Users/mike/work/dms-1.0-rb/dist/dms-1.0.zip
BUILD SUCCESSFUL
Total time: 2 seconds
```

This creates two files in the ~/work/dms-1.0-rb/dist directory: dms.jar and dms-1.0.zip. Because JAR files are compatible with the ZIP file format, the jar tool can be used to check the contents of the distribution ZIP file.

```
$ cd ~/work/dms-1.0-rb/dist
$ jar tf dms-1.0.zip
dms-1.0/
dms-1.0/LICENSE
dms-1.0/README
dms-1.0/bin/
dms-1.0/bin/index.bat
dms-1.0/bin/index.sh
dms-1.0/bin/indexAll.bat
dms-1.0/bin/indexAll.sh
dms-1.0/bin/search.bat
dms-1.0/bin/search.sh
dms-1.0/doc/
dms-1.0/doc/Example1.html
dms-1.0/doc/Example2.html
dms-1.0/doc/Example3.html
dms-1.0/lib/
dms-1.0/lib/dms.jar
dms-1.0/vendor/
dms-1.0/vendor/lib/
dms-1.0/vendor/lib/Tidy.jar
dms-1.0/vendor/lib/lucene-1.3.jar
```

Testing the Distribution Contents

We've created a distribution file, but does it contain all the necessary files? It would be good to know for sure before we start shipping this release. We could punt for now, knowing that when we deliver the release to QA they'll poke and prod it for us. If an important file is missing, the phone will ring.

But you'd like to limit the number of times your phone rings. We have a few strategies for verifying that the distribution file contains all the right stuff.

- *Compare the file contents.* You could run the diff command or an equivalent to compare the contents of the unzipped distribution file against the files in the release branch directory. You'll need to be smart about how you do that given that the distribution contains a subset of files from the release branch, but it's possible.

- *Run the application.* This involves unzipping the distribution file and running a script that you know will fail if the distribution contents aren't intact. That is, you could do exactly what the customer will do once they've installed the distribution.

- *Run the tests.* Even though the tests aren't in the distribution file, you could, through some CLASSPATH mangling, run the tests in the release branch against the production classes in the dms.jar file of the distribution.

Each of these options verifies something different, so ideally you should run through all of them to get the most confidence. Running the application might be easiest option, if you know what should happen as a result. But it's only easiest the first time—the visual inspection required will get old pretty quickly. If we use the existing tests, both running and verifying the distribution will be automated.

"But wait!" you say. "Didn't you just tell me not to include the tests in the release? How can I run what's not there?" Ah, that's the neat part about automating this using Ant. We can arrange to run the code in the distribution file and the tests from our release branch. Watch....

Fake an Install

First, unzip the distribution file from the release branch directory into ~/testinstall. We're effectively doing what a customer would do during installation, though in a different directory.

```
$ mkdir ~/testinstall
$ cd ~/testinstall
$ unzip ~/work/dms-1_0-rb/dist/dms-1_0.zip
Archive:  /Users/mike/work/dms-1_0-rb/dist/dms-1_0.zip
 creating: dms-1_0/
inflactin: dms-1_0/LICENSE
inflating: dms-1_0/README
 creating: dms-1_0/bin/
...
```

This creates a ~/testinstall/dms-1_0 directory that contains everything a customer would see.

Extract the JAR File

Next, "unjar" the dms.jar file in the distribution. This isn't necessary to run the software, but we'd like to use the existing build.xml file in the release branch directory to run the tests. It expects the production class files to be in a directory, not in a JAR file. So by expanding the JAR file using the jar command, you get a directory structure containing the production class files.

```
$ cd ~/testinstall/dms-1.0/lib
$ jar xvf dms.jar
  created: com/
  created: com/pragprog/
  created: com/pragprog/dms/
extracted: com/pragprog/dms/HtmlDocument.class
extracted: com/pragprog/dms/Indexer.class
extracted: com/pragprog/dms/Logger.class
extracted: com/pragprog/dms/Search.class
```

Now the production classes that get shipped in the distribution are sprawled out in the ~/testinstall/dms-1.0/lib directory. Their corresponding test classes are under the release branch directory ~/work/dms-1.0-rb/build/test.

Test the Distribution Classes

We need to run the test target of build.xml that's in the release branch directory. But we don't want to test the production classes in the release branch. Instead, we want to test the production classes in the distribution file we just unpacked. Because we stuck to sound design principles when we wrote our build script, we can override build directories by setting Ant properties on the command line. Run the test by typing

```
$ cd ~/work/dms-1.0-rb
$ ant test -Dbuild.prod.dir=/Users/mike/testinstall/dms-1.0/lib
-Dvendor.lib.dir=/Users/mike/testinstall/dms-1.0/vendor/lib
Buildfile: build.xml
prepare:
compile:
compile-tests:
test:
[junit] Testsuite: com.pragprog.dms.DocumentTest
[junit] Tests run: 2, Failures: 0, Errors: 0, Time elapsed: 0.519 sec

[junit] Testsuite: com.pragprog.dms.SearchTest
[junit] Tests run: 2, Failures: 0, Errors: 0, Time elapsed: 1.184 sec
BUILD SUCCESSFUL
Total time: 5 seconds
```

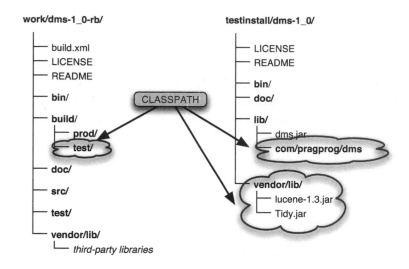

Figure 4.6: TESTING THE RELEASE

Notice that we overrode the location for production classes using the -Dbuild.prod.dir option. We also overrode the location for vendor libraries using -Dvendor.lib.dir. This means we're running the tests in the release branch directory against the production classes and vendor libraries in the unpacked distribution directory. The compile and compile-tests targets did nothing because all the class files are up-to-date. We're just using what we already have.

Figure 4.6 shows what the Java CLASSPATH includes when you run the test target with these options.

By testing across directories like this we're fairly sure that the distribution is ready for prime time. If the phone starts ringing off the hook, then we'll need to come up with another way to verify that the goods we're delivering are indeed good.

4.5 Tagging the Release

After you've done your best to ensure that the distribution file is golden, the next step in the release procedure is to tag the current contents of the release branch directory. This not only

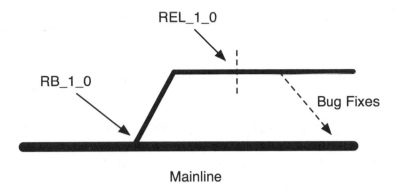

Figure 4.7: TAGGING THE RELEASE

creates an audit of all the files in the release, it also effectively gives you a time machine. At any time in the future you can use the release tag to check out the code used to generate this release. Tag the current contents of the release branch directory as REL_1_0 by typing

```
$ cd ~/work/dms-1_0-rb
$ cvs tag REL_1_0
cvs tag: Tagging .
T LICENSE
...
```

Using the cvs tag command to tag the release is different from the cvs rtag command used earlier. The cvs tag command tags the revisions of files in the repository that match what's checked out in the local directory. This way, if developers have checked in new changes while we've been off building, packaging, and testing, those changes won't be tagged. We want the tag to reflect what's actually in the release.

Figure 4.7 shows the tags now in the CVS repository. Between applying the RB_1_0 branch tag and the REL_1_0 release tag, we were preparing for the release and generating the distribution file. Now that we've officially generated a release in the repository by creating a release tag, we're ready to hand off the release to the QA team. If they report any bugs, we'll fix files in the release branch before merging them onto the mainline.

4.6 Handing Off the Release

The last step in our release procedure is to deliver it to the customer. Since we're just delivering to QA, it's as easy as copying the distribution file to a shared directory:

```
$ cp ~/work/dms-1_0-rb/dist/dms-1_0.zip /Users/Shared/releases
```

We'll look at other slightly more involved deployment scenarios in the next chapter. For now, the key point is that we have a distribution file. Where we choose to put that file—either locally or remotely—is another thing altogether.

4.7 Automating the Release Procedure

"Wait just one second," I hear folks saying. "Where's the automation in all of this? Our fingertips are raw from all the typing we've been doing on the command line, and we've learned that there's no repeatability to be gained by typing in a sequence of commands on the command line. So why are we doing all this manually and not automating it from the start?"

Well, before you can automate a procedure, you need to be able to run through it manually. That is, you can't teach this computer to do something before knowing how to do it yourself. So here's the good news you've been waiting for: The computer is going to generate our *next* release for us. That's right—anything you can do on the command line, the computer can do better once you teach it how.

Recapping What We Did

Let's review the steps we went through to generate our first release on the command line.

1. Test the contents of the mainline directory.
2. Create a release branch.
3. Check out the release branch.
4. Build and test the release branch.
5. Create a distribution file for the release.
6. Test the distribution file contents.
7. Tag the release.
8. Hand off the distribution file to QA.

This sequence of steps is our release procedure. It's a lot of work. And if we have to do all those things every time we cut a release, we won't want to cut a release very often. When we do, we'll likely mess something up because following detailed instructions is prone to boredom and error.

Scripting the Release Procedure

But all is not lost. Take a quick look back over those steps. The one variable in the whole equation is the version number. This week it's version 1.0, and next week perhaps we'll be ready with version 1.1. This means we can automate this entire release procedure in two scripts.

You do steps 1–4 every time you want to create a new release branch. Once you have a release branch, steps 5–8 generate a release on that branch. For example, you might create multiple releases from the same 1.0 release branch with each release containing a bug fix. That is, you run these two procedures at different intervals.

Figure 4.8 on the following page shows a push-button script called release_branch.sh that creates the release branch (steps 1–4). To create a release branch for the 1.1 release, type

```
$ sh release_branch.sh 1.1
```

Figure 4.9 on page 97 shows a script called release_generate.sh that generates the release from the release branch (steps 5–8). To generate a distribution file for release 1.1, type

```
$ sh release_generate.sh 1.1
```

Both of these scripts assume that you have the CVSROOT environment variable set to your CVS repository. Together they run through all eight steps of the release procedure, based on the specified version number, just like we did on the command line. If the build step that runs the tests fails in either script, then the release is not built.

Obviously, using a Unix shell script isn't the only way to automate the release procedure. You could use a Windows batch file, an Ant build file, or even some more powerful scripting language. Likewise, your release procedure will be different if you aren't using CVS. How you get to an automated

```bash
#!/bin/bash
if [ $# -eq 0 ]
then
  echo "usage: release_branch.sh <version>"
  exit 1
fi
VERSION=$1
NAME=dms
RELEASE=$NAME-$VERSION
WORK_DIR=$HOME/work
# 1. Test the mainline
cd $WORK_DIR
rm -rf $NAME
cvs co $NAME
cd $NAME
if ! ant test
then
  echo "Mainline test failed!"
  exit 1
fi
# 2. Create a release branch
cd $WORK_DIR/$NAME
cvs rtag -b RB_$VERSION $NAME
# 3. Check out the release branch
cd $WORK_DIR
cvs co -r RB_$VERSION -d $RELEASE-rb $NAME
# 4. Build and test the release branch
cd $WORK_DIR/$RELEASE-rb
if ! ant test
then
  echo "Release branch test failed!"
  exit 1
fi
```

dms/bin/release_branch.sh

Figure 4.8: CREATE A RELEASE BRANCH SCRIPT

release procedure is irrelevant. Getting there somehow is what's important.

4.8 Generating Daily Distributions

Any time you have a push-button script, you don't necessarily have to push a button to make it go. You can just as easily schedule the button to be pushed by a computer.

For example, right now we cut an official release by manually running a script. Between official releases, it might be convenient to automatically create daily internal releases. This is handy in the event that someone on the project wants to run the latest and greatest code but they don't want to go through

```
#!/bin/bash
if [ $# -eq 0 ]
then
  echo "usage: release_generate.sh <version>"
  exit 1
fi
VERSION=$1
NAME=dms
RELEASE=$NAME-$VERSION
WORK_DIR=$HOME/work
TEST_DIR=$HOME/testinstall
# 5. Create a distribution file
cd $WORK_DIR/$RELEASE-rb
ant -buildfile package.xml -Dversion=$VERSION
# 6. Test the distribution contents
cd $TEST_DIR
unzip $WORK_DIR/$RELEASE-rb/dist/$RELEASE.zip
cd $TEST_DIR/$RELEASE/lib
jar xvf $NAME.jar

cd $WORK_DIR/$RELEASE-rb
if ! ant test \
    -Dbuild.prod.dir=$TEST_DIR/$RELEASE/lib \
    -Dvendor.lib.dir=$TEST_DIR/$RELEASE/vendor/lib
then
  echo "Distribution test failed!"
  exit 1
fi
# 7. Tag the release
cd $WORK_DIR/$RELEASE-rb
cvs tag REL_$VERSION
# 8. Hand off the distribution file
cp $WORK_DIR/$RELEASE-rb/dist/$RELEASE.zip /Users/Shared/releases
```

dms/bin/release_generate.sh

Figure 4.9: GENERATE A RELEASE SCRIPT

the build process. These releases aren't for the faint of heart, mind you, as they are created from the mainline of our repository and therefore may contain incomplete features.

Figure 4.10 on the following page shows the release_daily.sh script. When this script runs, it puts a distribution file in a dated directory under /Users/Shared/releases/daily. And because you don't want to run it by hand every day, schedule the script with cron on Unix or with at on Windows. After the first three days you'll have the following directories, for example:

```
$ ls /Users/Shared/releases/daily
310304-Wednesday
010404-Thursday
020404-Friday
```

```bash
#!/bin/bash

VERSION=$1
NAME=dms
RELEASE=$NAME-$VERSION
WORK_DIR=$HOME/work
DATE=`date +%d%m%y-%A`
DATED_DIR=/Users/Shared/releases/daily/$DATE
# 1. Check out the project
cd $WORK_DIR
rm -r $RELEASE-daily
cvs co -d $RELEASE-daily $NAME
# 2. Build and test the project
cd $RELEASE-daily
if ! ant test
then
  exit 1
fi
# 3. Create a distribution file
ant -buildfile package.xml -Dversion=$VERSION
# 4. Drop the release in the dated directory
mkdir -p $DATED_DIR
cp $WORK_DIR/$RELEASE-daily/dist/$RELEASE.zip $DATED_DIR
```

dms/bin/release_daily.sh

Figure 4.10: DAILY RELEASE SCRIPT

Each of these directories contains a distribution file named for the version we're currently working toward. For example, if you're working on version 2.0, then each directory would contain a distribution file called dms-2.0.zip built from the current contents of the CVS repository. For convenience, you may want to create a symbolic link that always points to the current distribution file. Anybody can copy a distribution file and install it just as a customer will when it's officially released.

What We Just Did

We took a step-by-step manual release procedure and automated it so that it's easy to generate releases. Simply by pushing a button—running a script—we're able to generate consistent and repeatable releases. Anyone on our team can cut a release whenever we're ready to give our customers new features (or bug fixes). In the next chapter, we'll use automation to install and deploy new releases.

Chapter 5

Installation and Deployment

Putting our software in a user's hands is a watershed moment for any project. Too many projects unfortunately never see the light of day. We can increase our potential for success by generating frequent releases that can also be easily installed. In this chapter, we'll travel the last mile to our end-users.

5.1 Delivering the Goods

The ultimate goal in generating a release is to deliver the resulting distribution file to *end-users*—anyone from the guy down the hall to his grandmother living in the boonies. And it would be nice to be able to do this automatically. *end-users*

You can automate the delivery of the distribution to end-users in a variety of ways. This usually involves a bit of scripting, either by adding steps to your release script or by writing a separate script to push out the distribution file.

If users download the application over the web, then automation may be as simple as copying the distribution file to a shared drive or using FTP to transfer it to a server. Then you'd need to make sure that your public web site has a page that includes a hyperlink to the latest distribution file.

Alternatively, you might ship physical CDs to users. The release script might then include additional actions that walk you through the procedure of creating a master image, burning it onto a master CD, and firing up the CD duplicator.

5.2 Installing the Standard Distribution File

Regardless of their location, from our perspective every end-user wants the same thing: to use what's inside the distribution file. Installing it is simply a means to an end, so we need to make installing our software as painless as possible.

Let's assume, for example, that somehow an end-user has obtained a copy of the distribution ZIP file for version 1.0 of the *DMS* application. In other words, they have a file called dms-1_0.zip in their home directory. Before they can experience the cutting-edge world of document indexing and searching, they need to install the application. Because the distribution file is packaged in a ZIP format, the installation process is simple: unzip it. To do that, they change into their home directory and type

```
$ unzip dms-1_0.zip
Archive:   dms-1_0.zip
   creating: dms-1_0/
  inflating: dms-1_0/LICENSE
  inflating: dms-1_0/README
   creating: dms-1_0/bin/
  inflating: dms-1_0/bin/index.bat
  inflating: dms-1_0/bin/index.sh
  inflating: dms-1_0/bin/indexAll.bat
  inflating: dms-1_0/bin/indexAll.sh
  inflating: dms-1_0/bin/search.bat
  inflating: dms-1_0/bin/search.sh
   creating: dms-1_0/doc/
  inflating: dms-1_0/doc/Example1.html
  inflating: dms-1_0/doc/Example2.html
  inflating: dms-1_0/doc/Example3.html
   creating: dms-1_0/lib/
  inflating: dms-1_0/lib/dms.jar
   creating: dms-1_0/vendor/
   creating: dms-1_0/vendor/lib/
  inflating: dms-1_0/vendor/lib/Tidy.jar
  inflating: dms-1_0/vendor/lib/lucene-1.3.jar
```

That's the entire installation process! Armed with WinZip, even Grandma can handle that one. She'll likely also appreciate that all the files for version 1.0 of the *DMS* application were placed under the dms-1_0 directory. This makes it easy to find everything. Using the version number in the directory name also prevents the next release from overwriting the directory containing the previous release.

For some of our Java applications, unzipping a distribution file might be a sufficient installation process. All the files

explode onto the user's disk and then the user consults a
README file for further instructions. For example, to start
indexing and searching documents, they type

```
$ cd dms-1.0/bin
$ indexAll.bat
$ search.bat programmers vi emacs
```

This is where the location independence of the scripts and
batch files pays off. Without any additional installation steps,
these programs can find directories and dependent libraries
relative to the current working directory. Out of the box the
software just works, delighting our users. Indeed, unless
there's a problem, you may never hear from them again.

5.3   Troubleshooting by Phone

OK, so in reality you may be lucky enough to never hear
from *most* users. They unzip the distribution file, follow any
instructions in the README, and before long they've built
their own searching empire around using your humble *DMS*
application.

The users you do hear from, however, will often have installation problems that really hurt your brain. Some of these
same people couldn't pour water from a boot if the instructions were on the heel. Giving them better written installation
instructions simply won't help. Consider this fictional story,
which may sound frighteningly familiar:

> **Just Another Day in Tech Support**
> *by You*, Senior Programmer and Technical Support Jockey
>
> So there I was, heads-down in a Zen-like programming state
> that computers fear. The code was streaming from my
> fingertips, the compiler was laboring under the load, all the
> tests were passing in a green bar that could illuminate a small
> village...and then the phone rang. When I finally snapped back
> into reality, I remember the conversation going something like
> this:
>
> *Customer*: Hello. I'm a customer with deep pockets and a
> shallow memory. I just installed *DMS*, but it doesn't work?!
>
> *Me*: Strange. Our download stats say it's a banner day for our
> bank account, and you're the first to report a problem.

Customer: Well, it worked just great after I installed it, but when I run a search now I get a NoSuchMethodException.

Me: OK, but this didn't happen the first time you ran it. So what changed between installing it and running it now?

Customer: I haven't changed anything. I installed it yesterday and it worked, but today it's broken.

Me: Very interesting. Well, a NoSuchMethodException is typically a symptom of using an incompatible version of Java. *DMS* requires Java 1.4.*x*. You're running that version, right?

Customer: Of course. And it worked yesterday, so....

Me: And you obviously didn't change anything between then and now. So, uh, you're probably, um, running the correct Java version. Let's just, er, check. Please type in java -version.

Customer: OK. (Click, click...pause) Oops! It says java version 1.3.1. Did I mention that just this morning I was messing around with my JAVA_HOME environment variable?

Me: Funny that. OK, please change your JAVA_HOME back to your installation of Java version 1.4.1.

Customer: OK. Done!

Me: Great. Does it work now?

Customer: Nope, it still doesn't work. Now when I try to index documents it says it can't obtain a lock on my index directory.

Me: OK, at least we're making progress. Do you see a directory called index in your DMS_HOME directory?

Customer: Yes, I see that directory. Oh, that reminds me. Right after changing my JAVA_HOME this morning, I accidentally deleted that index directory. I lost a goodly amount of work. Major bummer, indeed. So after re-creating the index directory, I changed its permissions so I wouldn't accidentally delete it again.

Me: Ah. I'm sure that it's just a (cough) coincidence that you fiddled with the permissions of that directory and now the software doesn't work. It's a long shot, but can you check that you have read and write permission on your index directory?

(Long pause with muffled profanity.)

Customer: Just how much is this support call gonna cost me?

> After hanging up the phone, I leaned back in my chair, took a few deep breaths, and wished I could have the last 15 minutes of my life back. What a waste of my time. It'll take another half hour to get back into the programming zone.

If you've ever worked in a small shop, then you've probably lived this story. If you're working in a shop with a full-fledged tech support department, then somebody else is living it for you. And many of the tech support calls seem to go the same way: the wrong version of Java, a fatal change in the directory structure, or a minor configuration error. You might think you can keep on top of it all by creating checklists for troubleshooting these problems quickly. Then when the phone rings a dedicated tech support person walks meticulously through the checklist until—bingo!—the problem is found.

But what if you didn't need a technical support department after all, or at least not one that spends its time solving these nagging problems? Assume that you could come up with a checklist that diagnoses a large portion of installation problems. And instead of reading it over the phone to customers, you gave them the checklist when they had installation problems. You certainly wouldn't be the first project to do that. But what if instead of asking them to *read* the checklist, you asked them to *run* the checklist?

5.4 Troubleshooting with Diagnostic Tests

If the same installation problem crops up for two or more users, it's trying to tell us something. The installation process may be too complicated for a person to follow accurately and needs to be simplified in the next release. But we're still not home free. Undetected configuration changes after installation, such as we learned with the JAVA_HOME environment variable in the tech support story, can cause problems. Bundling the correct version of Java with our application is an option, but we can't escape the possibility of human error. All we can do is work to minimize it with good automation.

The standard response is to give all users a troubleshooting checklist, add all known installation issues to a FAQ, and hope for the best. But we can do better. As they said when they rebuilt The Six Million Dollar Man: "We have the technology." Indeed, our troubleshooting checklist is screaming for automation in the form of diagnostic tests.

Writing a Diagnostic Test

You're already using JUnit to write unit tests for your application. Those tests compare an expected value with an actual value, and if the values don't match, the test fails. When a unit test fails, you know something has gone haywire in your code. Unfortunately, you know something has gone haywire with a user's installation only when the phone rings.

What if you could put JUnit to work helping users diagnose when and why something has gone wrong with their installation? Figure 5.1 on the next page shows a JUnit test called InstallTests that defines two test methods.

- testJavaVersion checks the `java.version` system property to verify that version 1.4.*x* of Java is running.

- testIndexDirectory locates the installation directory using the `dms.dir` system property passed into the test when it's run. Then it verifies that a subdirectory called index exists with read and write permissions for the user running the test.

This simple diagnostic test might not seem like much. It checks a system property and a directory. And yet it can diagnose all the problems uncovered during the tech support phone conversation, and *much* more quickly. Now you just need a way to distribute it to users in their time of need.

Fielding Diagnostic Tests

When users experience problems, you need a way to drop diagnostic tests into their troubled installation. You could just always include tests in the standard distribution, but depending on the size of the distribution file and the frequency of problems, this may be overkill.

An alternative approach is to make a separate test distribution file available to users on demand. The release procedure we automated in the previous chapter sets us up to do just that. It creates a file called dms-1_0-tests.zip that contains all

```
package com.pragprog.dms.selftest;
import java.io.File;
import java.io.IOException;
import junit.framework.TestCase;
public class InstallTests extends TestCase {
  public void testJavaVersion() {
    String version = System.getProperty("java.version");
    assertTrue("Incompatible Java version. " +
      "Requires version 1.4.x, but found " + version,
      version.startsWith("1.4"));
  }
  public void testIndexDirectory() throws IOException {
    File dmsDir = getDirectory("dms.dir");
    File indexDir = new File(dmsDir, "index");
    assertDirectoryExists(indexDir);
    assertDirectoryReadable(indexDir);
    assertDirectoryWritable(indexDir);
  }
  void assertDirectoryExists(File dir) throws IOException {
    assertNotNull(dir);
    assertTrue("Directory doesn't exist: " + dir.getCanonicalPath(),
      dir.exists());
  }
  void assertDirectoryReadable(File dir) throws IOException {
    assertTrue("Directory not readable: " + dir.getCanonicalPath(),
      dir.canRead());
  }
  void assertDirectoryWritable(File dir) throws IOException{
    assertTrue("Directory not writable: " + dir.getCanonicalPath(),
      dir.canWrite()),
  }
  File getDirectory(String propertyName) {
    String dirName = System.getProperty(propertyName);
    assertNotNull("'" + propertyName + "' not defined", dirName);
    return new File(dirName);
  }
}
```

dms/test/com/pragprog/dms/selftest/InstallTests.java

Figure 5.1: INSTALLATION DIAGNOSTIC TEST

the tests in our build/test directory and a script to run the tests. This is in addition to creating the standard dms-1_0.zip distribution file.

When users notice a problem, you ask them to download the test distribution file and install it over the top of their standard distribution. That is, if they've installed version 1.0 of *DMS* in their home directory, then they would unzip the file dms-1_0-tests.zip in their home directory by typing

```
$ cd $HOME
$ unzip dms-1_0-tests.zip
Archive: dms-1_0-tests.zip
  inflating: dms-1_0/bin/selftest.bat
  inflating: dms-1_0/bin/selftest.sh
  inflating: dms-1_0/lib/dms-tests.jar
  inflating: dms-1_0/vendor/lib/junit-3.8.jar
```

Because the contents of this ZIP file are also under a directory with the same name as the standard distribution, the test-related files are expanded into the standard distribution directory. Think of it as adding a testing layer to the standard distribution, as shown in Figure 5.2 on the facing page.

Running the Diagnostic Tests

Now the user is ready to sic the diagnostic tests on their installation. To do that, they run the selftest script or batch file that was packaged in the test distribution file.

```
$ sh bin/selftest.sh
.F.F
Time: 0.092
There were 2 failures:
1) testJavaVersion(com.pragprog.dms.selftest.InstallTests)
   junit.framework.AssertionFailedError:
   Incompatible Java version. Requires version 1.4.x, but found 1.3.1
2) testIndexDirectory(com.pragprog.dms.selftest.InstallTests)
   junit.framework.AssertionFailedError:
   Directory not readable: /Users/somebody/dms-1_0/index
FAILURES!!!
Tests run: 2,  Failures: 2,  Errors: 0
```

Uh oh! The test explains that version 1.3.1 of Java is being used, but version 1.4.*x* is required. (And if the diagnostic tests can't be run because *no* version of Java is found, selftest.sh could politely inform the user of that.) What's more, this user doesn't have read permissions for their index directory. That's a 15-minute phone conversation reduced to pushing a button and reading the output.

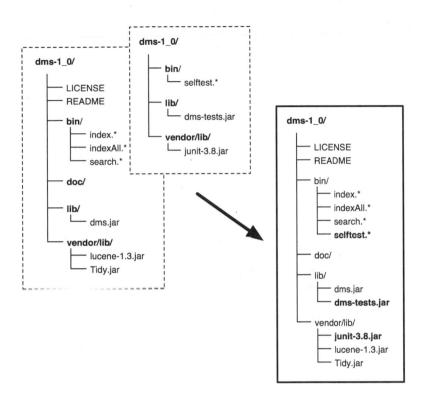

Figure 5.2: ADDING TESTS TO A STANDARD DISTRIBUTION

If the diagnostic messages are intuitive, then we hope the user can take the appropriate corrective action. Failing that, they send you the test output by email for analysis. That still takes far less of your time than troubleshooting by phone.

You know the application is back on solid ground when the user runs the tests and sees the welcomed OK message in the output.

```
$ sh bin/selftest.sh
..
Time: 0.082
OK (2 tests)
```

By putting these diagnostic tests in the field, you've essentially sent a tech support person to the user. That is, the test walks through the checklist in the same way you would on the phone.

```java
package com.pragprog.dms.selftest;
import junit.framework.Test;
import junit.framework.TestSuite;
public class AllTests {

  public static Test suite() {
    TestSuite suite = new TestSuite("DMS Selftests");
    suite.addTestSuite(InstallTests.class);
    suite.addTestSuite(ClasspathTests.class);
    // Add more diagnostic tests here
    return suite;
  }

  public static void main(String[] args) {
    junit.textui.TestRunner.run(suite());
  }
}
```

dms/test/com/pragprog/dms/selftest/AllTests.java

Figure 5.3: DIAGNOSTIC TEST SUITE

Writing a Diagnostic Test Suite

The two tests in InstallTests obviously can't diagnose all possible installation problems. But for now they cover the recurring installation problems we know about. So what happens when a new installation problem is reported by multiple users? You just add more diagnostic tests. Of course you have to make sure they don't have dependencies that would prevent the tests from running. Some example installation questions that tests can answer for users include

- Does the classpath (the `java.class.path` system property) include all the necessary files and directories in the proper order?

- Can the application get a database connection?

- Is the WAR or EAR file configured properly, and has it been installed in the appropriate directory?

- Is a required host or URL accessible?

As you write new tests, you'll likely create new JUnit test cases. To make it easy for the user to run all of the diagnostic tests en masse, put them all into a JUnit test suite. Figure 5.3 shows the AllTests test suite, which includes a new test case, called ClasspathTests.

The suite method adds the InstallTests and ClasspathTests test cases to a suite. This means that when the user runs the script selftest.sh, all the installation diagnostic tests will run.

```
$ ./bin/selftest.sh
...
Time: 0.075
OK (3 tests)
```

But why stop there? If the installation diagnostic tests all pass but the user is still experiencing a problem, then the more tests the better. And since you've already invested time writing unit tests that help you find problem during development, you might as well let them run in the field. To do that, you'd ask the user to run the AllUnitTests suite by, for example, passing an option to selftest.sh or by running another script.

Now we have a test suite that keeps paying us back. Every time it's run by a user, it automatically checks a bunch of important stuff. And if anything is out of whack, it fails with a detailed report of what went wrong. Better yet, no matter how many tests we add, the user still just types a single command to run them all.

5.5 Enhancing Your Installed Image

Let's face it, unzipping a distribution file isn't a sexy install process. It gets the job done, but it's not likely to attract the kind of attention that will make our software stand out from the crowd. It's also not a scriptable process—we have no way to add installation steps into the unzipping process. Once the distribution ZIP file has been expanded onto disk, any additional installation steps must be carried out manually by the user.

Thankfully, giving our users a professional-looking installer that also helps them follow all the installations steps correctly doesn't have to be difficult or expensive. Let's turn some heads by dressing up our installation process with a free installer that's rich with features and yet easy to use.

Installer Choices

NSIS is just one installer available to you. If you're not installing on Windows, have no fear. There are plenty of installers to go around.

The Mac OS X developer tools include the PackageMaker for creating a native installation package (.pkg) file. The ESP Package Manager* is an installer in the same price category as NSIS (free!) for native Unix formats. For cross-platform support, IzPack† is a Java-based installer that runs on any platform with a Java Virtual Machine.

If you have the budget for commercial installers, they offer lots of bells and whistles on various operating systems. For details on those, flip through almost any Java magazine or consult Google.

*http://www.easysw.com/epm
†http://www.izforge.com/izpack

Creating an Installer with NSIS

The Nullsoft Scriptable Install System[1] (NSIS) wraps applications in installers (and uninstallers) for Windows. If you've installed the Tomcat servlet engine on Windows, for example, you've used an NSIS-powered installer. Even though NSIS doesn't create installers for other operating systems, we'll use it as an example of what a great installer can do for you.

Write an NSIS Script

To create a NSIS installer, you write a script. This is just a text file that uses NSIS's powerful scripting language. The scripting language is very flexible and supports commands for automating all manner of installation tasks: creating directories, editing the registry, setting environment variables, and even rebooting the system. And yet we don't have to risk being electrocuted by all that power if we just need a basic installer.

---

[1]http://nsis.sourceforge.net

Figure 5.4 on the following page shows the first part of an NSIS script called dms.nsi that creates an installer/uninstaller for the *DMS* application. It does a bit more than a bare-bones installer, and we'll discuss why in a moment. But first, you might be looking at that strange syntax wondering how you'll write your own script from scratch. Well, here's the secret: You don't have to do that. The bulk of the dms.nsi script was generated using HM NIS Edit:[2] a free NSIS script editor. It has a script generation wizard that asks you basic questions about your installation process and then generates an NSIS script for you. Then you can tweak that script by hand in the editor to add more complex installation steps.

Just to give you a feel for the syntax, we'll walk through the high points of the script. The !insertmacro and Page commands near the top define the flow of the install/uninstall wizard pages. During installation, the user transitions through the following six wizard pages:

❶ Welcome the user to what's about to happen.

❷ Display the license agreement and prompt for acceptance before continuing.

❸ Let the user choose the destination directory.

❹ Show a custom page that prompts for user preferences.

❺ Install the files, showing a progress bar and the details of each installation step.

❻ Show a happy ending to put the user on their way.

Following the wizard page definitions, two installation sections are defined: AllSection (❼) and PostInstallSection (❽). These sections are executed during the installation step— the fifth wizard page.

The steps in AllSection (❼) do all the heavylifting. When you compile the script, this section compresses the files under the directory defined by the COMPRESS_DIR variable into an executable. When the executable is run on the user's machine, it will extract those files into the c:\Program Files\DMS-1.0 directory while preserving the directory structure. After all those

---

[2]http://hmne.sourceforge.net

```
!define PRODUCT_NAME "DMS-1.0"
!ifndef COMPRESS_DIR
!define COMPRESS_DIR "c:\test\dms-1.0"
!endif

Name "${PRODUCT_NAME}"
OutFile "Setup.exe"
InstallDir "$PROGRAMFILES\${PRODUCT_NAME}"

!include "MUI.nsh"

; Install Pages (1-6)
```
❶ `!insertmacro MUI_PAGE_WELCOME`
❷ `!insertmacro MUI_PAGE_LICENSE "${COMPRESS_DIR}\LICENSE"`
❸ `!insertmacro MUI_PAGE_DIRECTORY`
❹ `Page custom UserPrefsPage`
❺ `!insertmacro MUI_PAGE_INSTFILES`
❻ `!insertmacro MUI_PAGE_FINISH`
```
; Uninstall Pages (1-2)
!insertmacro MUI_UNPAGE_CONFIRM
!insertmacro MUI_UNPAGE_INSTFILES

!insertmacro MUI_LANGUAGE "English"
```
❼
```
Section "All Components" AllSection
  SetOutPath "$INSTDIR"
  File /r "${COMPRESS_DIR}\*.*"
  Call WritePropertyFile
SectionEnd
```
❽
```
Section -PostInstallSection
  WriteUninstaller "$INSTDIR\Uninstall.exe"
  CreateDirectory "$SMPROGRAMS\${PRODUCT_NAME}"
  CreateShortCut "$SMPROGRAMS\${PRODUCT_NAME}\Search.lnk" \
                 "$INSTDIR\bin\search.bat"
  CreateShortCut "$SMPROGRAMS\${PRODUCT_NAME}\Uninstall.lnk" \
                 "$INSTDIR\Uninstall.exe"
SectionEnd
```
❾
```
Section Uninstall
  RMDir /r "$INSTDIR"
  RMDir /r "$SMPROGRAMS\${PRODUCT_NAME}"
SectionEnd
```

dms/installer/dms.nsi

Figure 5.4: NSIS SCRIPT (PART 1)

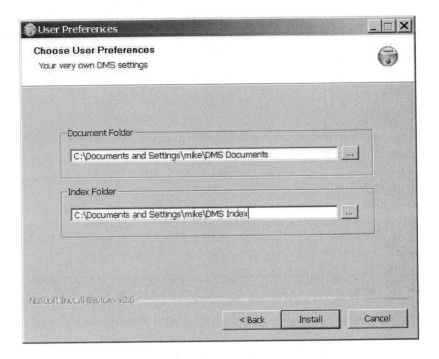

Figure 5.5: CUSTOM INSTALLATION WIZARD PAGE

files have been installed, the `WritePropertyFile` function is called. We'll explore that function a bit later.

`PostInstallSection` (❽), creates an uninstaller executable called Uninstall.exe. Running this executable causes the `Uninstall` section (❾) to be run. Shortcuts are also created in the `Start` menu for the user's convenience.

Design a Custom Installation Page

We'd like to go above and beyond the basic installation steps by adding a custom page that prompts the user for their personal configuration options. Say, for example, during installation we want the user to be able to choose two *DMS*-specific directories: a directory containing documents to index and an index directory. Designing custom pages is made easier with the InstallOptions Designer in HM NIS Edit. Figure 5.5 shows a custom page prompting for two directories.

```
      Function .onInit
        !insertmacro MUI_INSTALLOPTIONS_EXTRACT "UserPrefsPage.ini"
      FunctionEnd
❶    Function UserPrefsPage
        !insertmacro MUI_HEADER_TEXT "Choose User Preferences" \
                                    "Your very own DMS settings"
        !insertmacro MUI_INSTALLOPTIONS_DISPLAY "UserPrefsPage.ini"
      FunctionEnd
      Var DOC_DIR
      Var INDEX_DIR
❷    Function WritePropertyFile
        !insertmacro MUI_INSTALLOPTIONS_READ $DOC_DIR \
                  "UserPrefsPage.ini" "Field 2" "State"
        !insertmacro MUI_INSTALLOPTIONS_READ $INDEX_DIR \
                  "UserPrefsPage.ini" "Field 4" "State"
      FileOpen  $0 "$PROFILE\dms.properties" "w"
      FileWrite $0 "document.directory=$DOC_DIR$\r$\n"
      FileWrite $0 "index.directory=$INDEX_DIR$\r$\n"
      FileClose $0
      DetailPrint "Stored user preferences in $PROFILE\dms.properties"
      FunctionEnd
```

dms/installer/dms.nsi

Figure 5.6: NSIS SCRIPT (PART 2)

After the user has chosen directories, those preferences are stored in a file called dms.properties in a user-specific directory. If the properties file exists when *DMS* is run, the user's chosen directories will override the default directories. Storing this file on a per-user basis in a separate directory makes it safe to upgrade to a new *DMS* version without losing user preferences.

Figure 5.6 shows the second part of the dms.nsi script that defines custom functions. The UserPrefsPage function (❶) displays the custom page shown in Figure 5.5 on the page before. The WritePropertyFile function (❷) captures values supplied by the user and then writes those values in the dms.properties file. For example, given that the user "mike" enters the values shows in Figure 5.5 on the preceding page, then C:\Documents and Settings\mike\dms.properties would contain

```
document.directory=C:\Documents and Settings\mike\DMS Documents
index.directory=C:\Documents and Settings\mike\DMS Index
```

Being able to script extensions into the installation process is important because it allows you to automate custom steps. Consider how you might extend this to automate the installation of more complex applications. For example, a custom wizard page could ask for information about your web server and database, and the install step could then expand an application configured on the fly into the appropriate directory of your application server.

Generate an Executable

After writing the dms.nsi installer script, you need to compile it. To run the compiler, you can either right-click the script file and choose "Compile NSIS Script" or compile the script directly in the HM NIS Edit editor. These options work well to test the script as you're writing it, but at some point you need to automate the compile step. That's when running the NSIS compiler (MakeNSIS.exe) from the command line comes in handy. To compile the script, type

```
% MakeNSIS dms.nsi
```

The compiler parses the script and creates an installer and an uninstaller: the Setup.exe file and the Uninstall.exe file.

Running the compiler from the command line gives us a lot of automation options. Suppose, for example, we want to use the distribution ZIP file as the source of files for the installer. That is, instead of trying to locate all the individual files that will go into the installer, we want to unzip the distribution ZIP file and put all those files into the installer. This helps keep both distribution files consistent—the dms-1_0.zip file and the Setup.exe will contain the same files.

To do that, you need to override the COMPRESS_DIR variable to point to the directory containing the files that go into the installer. First, unzip dms-1_0.zip into the c:\install directory. Then, compress all those files into the installer executable by typing

```
% makensis /DCOMPRESS_DIR=c:\install\dms-1_0 dms.nsi
```

In other words, overriding variables on the command line lets you vary the directory names from version to version without having to edit the NSIS script. This means you could run

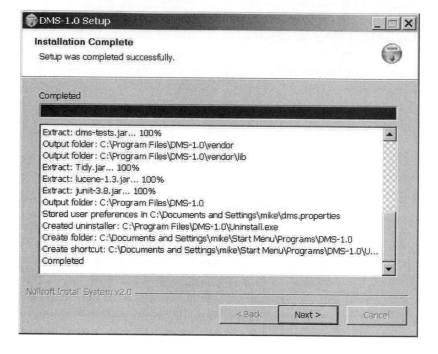

Figure 5.7: A SUCCESSFUL INSTALL

the NSIS compiler every time you run the release script to generate an installer for the new release, simply by passing in the name of a version-specific directory.

Ship It!

Compile the NSIS script, and we end up with a self-contained (yet surprisingly small!) executable file called Setup.exe. That's all you need to give to end-users. You could provide a link to it on your web site, burn it on a CD, or choose any of a number of delivery options.

To install *DMS*, users simply run the Setup.exe file and answer any questions posed by the wizard. Figure 5.7 shows the installer in action.

Customers might also like to take advantage of automation. Say, for example, they want to install *DMS* on a number of machines, all with the same installation directory and configuration options. Going through the installer wizard for each machine will definitely slow them down and could introduce inconsistencies. Thankfully, NSIS supports silent installation by allowing default values to be used for such things as message boxes and configuration information to be passed in with command-line options.

Now we have an installer that presents itself well to the user. Moreover, it automates installation steps and verifies configuration options for improved accuracy. All this means you'll spend less time diagnosing installation problems, and your customers will love you for it.

5.6 Deploying Hosted Applications

Some Java applications need to be deployed into a server. That installation process involves slightly more than unzipping a distribution file in a user's home directory. We might be tempted to stop short here with automation, choosing to automate only the low-hanging installation fruit. But as the complexity of deployment increases, so does the manual workload and the potential for error. This is one area where automation can really pay off by helping you deploy new releases quickly and accurately.

Deploying hosted J2EE applications is made easier through the use of standardized, self-contained deployment modules—WAR and EAR files. These deployment modules contain build outputs such as Java class files, dependent JAR files, and deployment descriptors that declare how the deployed application interacts with the server.

Let's briefly walk through some techniques for automating the deployment of a J2EE application.

Creating Deployment Modules

Creating WAR and EAR files is part of the build process. So, because we're already using Ant as our build tool, we'd add additional targets to our build file that generate these build artifacts. Those build targets would use the <war> and <ear> Ant tasks to automate the assembly of WAR and EAR files from the files in our project directory. See [HL02] for details on how to use these Ant tasks.

Then our release script could invoke these targets to generate WAR or EAR files ready for deployment. It might also generate a ZIP distribution file that contained all the deployment modules ready for distribution to internal or external users. In other words, using Ant allows you to re-create deployment modules consistently just like any other build artifact.

Deploying the Application

In general, deploying a new version of a J2EE application involves shutting down the server, dropping a new WAR or EAR file in the appropriate server directory, and then restarting the server. Many servers even support hot deployment so you don't have to go through the restart procedure. This deployment procedure can be automated.

Hot Deploy the Application

If your server supports hot deployment, the simplest automated deployment technique may be to copy or file-transfer the deployment files into a "hot" directory. Of course Ant includes *<copy>*, *<scp>*, and *<ftp>* tasks, but these operations are just as easy to script. You can use the ftp command, for example, to upload a local file to a remote server.

The ftp command has many variants, but one approach that works equally well on Unix or Windows is to command it through file redirection. Let's say, for example, your application server is running on a machine called enoch. It hot deploys applications placed in the /server/webapps directory. To upload and deploy a new version of the dms.war file, type

```
ftp -n enoch < upload.ftp
```

Once an FTP connection is established, the following sequence of commands in the upload.ftp file are fed into the FTP command interpreter:

```
user username password
binary
cd /server/webapps
put dms.war
```

This is low-tech, but it's automation at its finest because it's noninteractive and repeatable. When you want to deploy the dms.war module, simply run the ftp command from the command line or as a step in a script. Copying the module to a local or shared directory is equally easy to automate.

Build Your Own Hot Deploy

Many application servers include custom Ant tasks for deployment. For example, Tomcat includes Ant tasks for stopping an application, deploying files remotely through Tomcat's web interface, and then restarting the application. The following is an example target that uses Tomcat's custom *<deploy>* task to upload a local WAR file into a remote server:

```
<target name="deploy">
  <deploy url="${tomcat.manager.url}"
    username="${tomcat.manager.username}"
    password="${tomcat.manager.password}"
    path="/${webapp.name}"
    war="file:${warfile.path}"/>
</target>
```

dms/installer/deploy.xml

Using Tomcat's custom Ant tasks you can build your own hot deployment script by chaining targets together, like this:

```
<target name="hot-deploy" depends="stop, undeploy, deploy, start" />
```

Deploying the application into the remote Tomcat server is now automated by running the deploy.xml build file, for example, which runs the hot-deploy target by default.

```
$ ant -buildfile deploy.xml
Buildfile: deploy.xml
stop:
  [stop] OK - Stopped application at context path /dms
undeploy:
  [undeploy] OK - Undeployed application at context path /dms
deploy:
  [deploy] OK - Deployed application at context path /dms
start:
  [start] OK - Started application at context path /dms
hot-deploy:
BUILD SUCCESSFUL
Total time: 2 seconds
```

The Tomcat web interface supports all the commands offered by the Ant tasks. This means you can command Tomcat to start an application by issuing an HTTP GET request that includes the start command as a URL parameter. So with a series of wget commands in a shell script, for example, you can automate the same hot deployment procedure as in the deploy.xml Ant script.

Practice on Stage

Before we put the latest version of our application in front of a live studio audience, we need to practice on stage. A staging server offers a production-like setting without the possibility of tomatoes being thrown if the application bombs. This is where QA gets to run their battery of acceptance tests before the application goes live.

Deploying to the staging server is both a test of your application and your deployment process. Make sure to use the same automation technique to deploy to the staging server as to deploy in the production server. This means the deployment scripts should be easy to configure between servers. In the case of an Ant script, this might be as simple as overriding the tomcat.manager.url property when the hot-deploy target is run.

Run a Production Sound Check

After QA has finally given the green light and the application is deployed onto the production server, it's time to run a last-minute sound check. This final test is just another step in a deployment script. We basically want to know if the correct version of the application has been deployed and is open for business.

One simple approach is to embed a diagnostic web page with every deployed web application. That page could include the current version number, among other things. Then you could write a trivial program that verifies that the version number on the page matches the version number just deployed. The last step of your deployment script runs this program as a sanity check against what it deployed. We'll explore more techniques for monitoring deployed applications in Section 6.4, *Checking Up on Your Web Application*, on page 136.

So, if you feel more at home in Ant than in a shell script or a batch file, then use Ant as a deployment tool. Otherwise, you can do all this same automation with a script. The goal is automation; how you get there isn't nearly as important.

Tackling Complex Deployments

"I wish deploying applications to my server were this easy," you say. "But our server doesn't have these deployment hooks to use for script-based automation." Indeed, some servers can be a challenge and require a bit more creativity than we've seen in this chapter. As just one example of that creative spirit in action, let's see how one team solved their server's deployment challenges.

Automating Deployments to WebSphere
by Scott Hasse, Isthmus Group, Inc.

My team was recently faced with the challenge of automating J2EE application builds and deployments from an existing ClearCase environment to a new WebSphere platform. There were several challenges that made the project interesting.

Deploying enterprise applications to WebSphere via the web administrative console can be an involved process, consisting of several configuration and resource mapping steps. To solve this problem, we used wsadmin, an IBM-provided command-line interface to WebSphere's JMX management features. As of WebSphere Application Server 5.1, you can either use JACL (a TCL variant) or Jython to script operations in wsadmin. Since we had some existing Python skills on the team, we opted to use Jython. An additional benefit was Jython's seamless integration with the extensive Java APIs.

Although using the wsadmin interface the first few times was not as easy as clicking buttons in the web administrative console, it eventually enabled us to automate even the finest detail of application deployments to WebSphere. We even found a built-in facility that allowed us to deploy an application manually one time and then capture the resulting command to an application-specific Jython deployment script to automate future deployments.

To actually perform the deployments, we created a main deploy script that is able to retrieve an EAR file with an arbitrary version or label out of ClearCase, run the Jython scripts embedded in the EAR file to ensure the application-specific resources are properly created, and deploy the application itself. The centralized script handles the task of stopping the application, removing the existing deployment, and starting the application after it has been (re)deployed.

This combination of solutions has allowed us to achieve a remarkable degree of process improvement and deployment automation. The amount of time developers have had to devote to making sure deployment goes well has been significantly reduced. The application infrastructure team can now do push-button deployments. Customer and QA platform confidence has increased dramatically.

Scott's story teaches us to look under our server's hood for deployment hooks. Another lesson is that automating complex deployment procedures often requires the power of a real scripting language. But once you overcome the challenges, deployment automation continues to pay for itself.

5.7 Auto-Updating Installed Applications

If updating installed software is automatic, then most of our users will always be running the latest and greatest version of our software. This means they'll benefit from bug fix releases, security patches, and new features.

If updating software is a manual step, however, then users will fall behind, and we'll potentially end up with every version of our software in the field. And when the tech support phone rings, our first question to the user will always be, "Are you running the latest version?" If they aren't, we'll ask them to install the latest version and call back if it doesn't fix their problem.

Ideally we want an auto-updater that checks for new updates on a schedule: daily, weekly, or monthly. Or perhaps it checks for updates every time the user runs the application, or every fifth time. At any rate, the user shouldn't have to remember to check for updates.

Writing a Custom Auto-Updater

At first blush, writing an auto-updater appears trivial. The algorithm goes something like this:

1. Trigger the update on a schedule or an event.

2. Programmatically hit a known web site URL that returns the current version number.

3. If the current version is greater than the installed version, then automatically download the current version.

4. Optionally show the user a dialog box explaining that a new version is available and that it should be installed.

5. Install the latest version.

You could probably implement the best-case scenario for the first few steps on a Friday afternoon. It's a fun exercise in network programming. The last step—upgrading an existing installation with the new version—can be tricky. Users expect auto-updates to be bullet-proof. They're running a perfectly good application, and we're asking them to update it. When it's all over, they should have a *better* application that also remembers everything they did in the previous version. It's not an unreasonable expectation.

But everyone has a horror story about a time when they let the computer update software for them. It takes only one of those experiences to make you never want to auto-update again. Don't expect building an auto-updater to be something you can pull off in a day at the end of a release cycle. You might get something working for the happy path, but your users might not be happy with the results.

We can't possibly build a realistic auto-updater in this chapter. Most auto-updaters are custom pieces of software that install applications with custom needs. Reusable solutions will likely emerge as auto-updating gradually becomes more prevalent. But just to whet your appetite, we'll write a simple auto-updater using a free technology: Java Web Start.

Auto-Updating with Java Web Start

Java Web Start[3] (JWS) lets you deploy applications directly from the web. You launch an application for the first time by using a web browser to access a special file on the software vendor's web site. The application is then automatically downloaded to your computer and starts running.

Each subsequent time you launch the application, behind the scenes JWS will check the web to see if a new version is available. If a new version isn't available or JWS can't contact the server to make a determination, the local version cached on your computer is used. If a new version is available, JWS will automatically download it and run the new version instead of the local version. This means you're automatically always using the most recent version available.

Know Your Limitations

Java Web Start sounds lovely, but you should keep a few important restrictions in mind. It works best in the following contexts:

- Your application is a Java GUI using Swing or SWT, and you intend to deploy it to a wide user base.

- Your application can be delivered as a set of JAR files. All application resources (e.g., configuration files) must be included in the JAR files and looked up using the services of the Java classloader.

- Your users have already installed (or they can tolerate installing) an appropriate version of the Java Runtime Environment (JRE). They need this to run JWS, which is bundled in recent JRE versions, and to run your downloaded application.

- By default, JWS runs applications in a secure "sandbox" with restricted access to local resources, such as the filesystem. If your application needs unrestricted access to these resources, then you'll need to digitally sign your JAR files.

---

[3]http://java.sun.com/products/javawebstart

```xml
<?xml version="1.0" encoding="UTF-8"?>
<jnlp spec="1.0+"
  codebase="http://www.yourdomain.com/products" href="DMS.jnlp" >
  <information>
    <title>DMS</title>
    <vendor>Your Company Name, Inc.</vendor>
    <description>Document Management System</description>
    <offline-allowed />
  </information>
  <resources>
    <j2se version="1.4+" />
    <jar href="dms.jar" />
    <jar href="lucene-1.3.jar" />
    <jar href="Tidy.jar" />
  </resources>
  <application-desc main-class="com.pragprog.dms.GUI" />
  <!-- If JARs are signed, allow to run wild. -->
  <security>
    <all-permissions />
  </security>
</jnlp>
```

dms/installer/DMS.jnlp

Figure 5.8: JAVA WEB START JNLP FILE

Write a JNLP File

To make software available over the web for users with JWS, you need to write a Java Network Launching Protocol (JNLP) file. This is the file users will access over the web, so it must be accessible through your web site. Figure 5.8 shows an example JNLP file for the *DMS* application.

Configure the Server Side

Next, put the JNLP file and the dms.jar file in a subdirectory called products in your web server's document root directory. With this in place, users can download and run *DMS* by pointing their web browser to

http://www.yourdomain.com/products/DMS.jnlp

Provided users have version 1.4.*x* of a JRE installed on their machine, that's all there is to it! They hit that web address, the dms.jar file is downloaded, and the main method in the com.pragprog.dms.GUI class is run.

Later, if you fix a bug and update the contents of dms.jar on your server, all users get that bug fix the next time they run *DMS*. You can also configure JWS to send only changed Java classes to the client, rather than the entire JAR file.

Notice that JWS doesn't address an important auto-update issue: How do you ensure that version-specific files and preferences from the prior version are migrated to the new version? This is custom programming that's likely to take more than an afternoon.

Java Web Start is one example of an auto-updater. It's not always the right tool for the job. If your application and users meet the criteria, then you'll want to dig deeper[4] into JWS. Otherwise, consider it a thought experiment for how you might benefit from an auto-update strategy.

What We Just Did

We started off by installing a distribution file using a low-tech installer: unzip. When our software didn't behave as expected in the field, we automated the troubleshooting process by installing and running diagnostic tests. Then we wrote an installer that gives our application a more professional look. We also explored automation techniques for deploying hosted applications. Finally, we deployed our application over the web and made sure its users are always running the latest and greatest version.

---

[4]http://lopica.sourceforge.net is a great resource for everything related to JWS.

Chapter 6

Monitoring

Writing quality code for each release takes your best efforts and attention. When you're focused on moving forward, you don't have time to keep checking the rearview mirror. Instead, you need to be actively notified when something demands your attention.

In this chapter we'll explore ways to use *triggered automation* to monitor builds and running programs. These are merely suggested monitoring techniques to help get you going. Feel free to color outside the lines and come up with other creative ways to monitor what's important to you. And make sure to have some fun along the way!

6.1 Monitoring Scheduled Builds

Knowing as soon as possible if a scheduled build has failed is important because it means you need to stop making changes until the build is fixed. Otherwise you're just throwing good work after bad. And fixing the build now will be easier than trying to fix it later when problems have compounded.

Way back in Section 3.4, *Sending Build Results via Email*, on page 64, we configured CruiseControl to send a spiffy email when the build fails. That's great, if everyone checks email. But what if you're at the beach?

Sending Build Results to Your Cell Phone

If your cell phone or pager can receive text messages, you don't need to be within reach of email to know when the build breaks. Indeed, text messaging has grown from something your teenager does with friends to an effective way to communicate with machines. That's right, you could be lounging on a tropical beach, soaking up warm rays, the ocean breeze fanning your sun-burned face...and then suddenly your mobile phone beeps.

OK, so that may not be the best thing for your vacation plans. But at least you'll know the rest of your programmer buddies are hard at work fixing the build. And that makes your refreshing drink taste that much better.

Add an Email Publisher to CruiseControl

Most providers of wireless phones and pagers assign an email address to each account that has a text messaging (SMS) feature. Sending build results to your cell phone (or your pager) is as easy as sending an email. To do that with CruiseControl, just define an additional publisher.

```
<email mailhost="your.smtp.host"
  returnaddress="cruisecontrol@clarkware.com"
  buildresultsurl="">
  <map alias="fred" address="3035551212@mobile.att.net" />
  <failure address="fred" reportWhenFixed="true" />
</email>
```

The *<email>* publisher sends a plain-text email to all registered recipients. In this example, when a build fails, Fred's mobile phone gives him a jolt. Then when the build has been fixed, Fred gets another message. Ah...now back to that tropical vacation.

You may recall that we used the *<htmlemail>* publisher when we initially set up CruiseControl. That publisher is still in use. We've just added the *<email>* publisher for those folks who also want the build status sent to their phone or pager, but not in an HTML format.

Broadcasting a Build RSS Signal

Back in Section 3.4, *Pulling Build History from a Web Page*, on page 67 we discussed using CruiseControl's optional web application to view the build history. That's useful for the casual build observer or while we're doing build archaeology. But you probably won't remember to go look at that web page as often as you should to notice build failures.

Rather than actively pulling information from a web site, we'd like to get it pushed to the desktop. RSS is becoming increasingly pervasive as a low-tech way to push information around. An RSS feed is an XML file that lives on a server. You point an RSS reader at the file, and each time the file is updated, your reader highlights the feed as having new information.

What advantage does using RSS have over sending the build status as email? Say you want to collect information from various sources on your project—including the status of all the latest builds—and display it like the dashboard in your car. An email just won't do. You need a way to push the build status to an application that can parse it in a standard way. That's where RSS really shines because it offers an easy way to aggregate multiple feeds into one consistent view.

Add an XSLT Publisher to CruiseControl

CruiseControl formats all its build logs as XML. Trust that you don't want to read those log files. They're not intended to be viewed by human eyes. But to a computer, those log files are quite attractive. Since RSS is just another XML format, through the power of XSLT we'll transform the XML build logs into an RSS build feed. To do that, add an XSLT publisher.

```
<XSLTLogPublisher
  directory="/Library/WebServer/Documents"
  outfilename="dmsbuildstatus.rss"
  xsltfile="buildstatus.xsl" />
```

The *<XSLTLogPublisher>* is another publisher defined within the *<publishers>* element of the CruiseControl config.xml file. It uses a custom XSLT stylesheet called buildstatus.xsl.[1] This

---

[1]Available at http://www.pragmaticprogrammer.com/sk/auto, the book's web site.

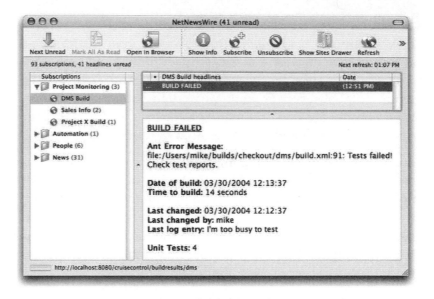

Figure 6.1: BUILD RESULTS VIA RSS

stylesheet transforms the last build log into a dmsbuildstatus.rss file in the build machine's web server directory.

Every time the build process runs, the RSS feed is updated. Anybody can get the latest build results by pointing their favorite RSS reader to a URL similar to the following:

```
http://buildmachine/dmsbuildstatus.rss
```

Figure 6.1 shows how the NetNewsWire[2] RSS reader displays a build failure RSS item. In this case, you may want more information than is contained in this summary. That's when CruiseControl's web application comes in handy. The hyperlink at the top of the RSS item gives you a quick link to the web page showing the complete build history.

6.2 Getting Feedback from Visual Devices

We've looked at several ways to radiate build information, either by pushing it via email, SMS, and RSS or by pulling it

---

[2]http://ranchero.com/netnewswire. This is a Mac product.

Joe Asks...
What If My Team Is Dislocated?

These days it's not uncommon for software to be built by teams distributed across the globe. For example, one team may be working in the United States and another team in India. In this scenario, the two teams are 12 hours apart in their work shifts. At the end of every shift, an implicit hand-off occurs. One team starts their programming day, and the other heads for home. At that transition point, the build needs to be in a stable state. This allows one team to quickly pick up where the other left off.

Building software is as much about communication as it is about writing code. When teams are dislocated by distance and time, communication will naturally suffer. Spreading the word that the system isn't successfully building by hanging out at the water cooler just won't work.

So dislocated teams have more to gain from monitoring builds from a common source because it provides a synchronization point. That is, everybody needs to know that they're starting with a successful build every morning. Being able to get feedback about the last build by looking at an RSS feed, or even an official web page, gives each team confidence to continue moving forward.

from a web page. But your team may already be inundated, or just plain bored, with information delivered this way. When that happens, you need to use something eye-popping and, well, *cool*. The health of your software is entirely too important to be ignored.

Let's get an eyeful of fun ideas by considering how one project is using visual devices[3] to radiate the status of their builds.

---

[3]Have a look at http://www.pragmaticautomation.com for more cool and effective feedback devices.

Figure 6.2: XFD BUILD MONITOR

eXtreme Feedback Devices
by Alberto Savoia, CTO, Agitar Software Inc.

To make sure that key project data that we want to monitor and act upon does not go unobserved, I've started to experiment with what I call eXtreme Feedback Devices (XFDs). XFDs are designed to call attention to themselves and the data they monitor. In order to do that the devices should be somewhat unique or, at the very least, placed in very visible and hard-to-miss locations.

Figure 6.2 shows a picture of one of my first XFD experiments, which is still used to this day. The display alternates between two full-screen "pages": One shows the number of open bugs, and the other shows the result of our continuous automated build and test cycles. The display is posted in a very visible and well-frequented area of our building: by the coffee and water cooler. Everyone in the company (including our CEO, VP of Marketing, and even the sales team) has made a habit of looking at it. Since I sit near the monitor, I hear people making comments about the metrics several times a day.

When a particularly challenging or important metric changes (from good to bad or otherwise) everybody notices: "We finally cleaned up all our P1 bugs!" or "Hey, who broke the build?" In addition to giving very useful status on our bugs and the builds, the visibility of the display creates some friendly peer pressure that gets people to act quickly to resolve any problems.

The cost of implementing this XFD is minimal since you probably have an old or unused PC that will be more than adequate for running the monitoring application. I spent about $500 for an LCD monitor and a wall-mounting bracket. The software (written in Java) polls our build machine (where we do continuous builds using CruiseControl) and our bug database (Bugzilla) and updates the results every few minutes. It took me only a couple of hours to write the software: ten minutes for the guts of the code and the rest to tweak the fonts and graphics layout to make it look good.

It's OK to break the build once in a while; it's actually a good sign that the tests are catching problems. But if it's important to get a build fixed as soon as possible, a Lava Lamp makes a great XFD. Figure 6.3 on the following page shows our dual-bubbly-lamp build monitor in action.

Since it takes a few minutes for the goo in the lamp to start bubbling (time enough to fix minor problems that should be fixed ASAP), the feedback mechanism matches the desired behavior: fix the problem before the lamp starts bubbling. In the original implementation of this XFD, I used a single red Lava Lamp since red is associated with problems and the objective was to keep it from bubbling. Developers, however, really liked looking at the bubbles, so I added a green lamp that is active when the build is not broken. This way one of the Lava Lamps is always going.

In order to turn an ordinary Lava Lamp into an XFD, I used a computer-driven wireless home automation system called FireCracker (www.x10.com). I wrote a small Java program that polls our intranet to check the build status and then interfaces with the X10 system through a wireless device to turn the lamp on and off.

- Cost of Lava Lamps: $40 for 2
- Cost of X10 devices: $60
- Using Java and lava to keep the builds clean: priceless

Based on my experience, I'm 100 percent sold on the idea of eXtreme Feedback Devices. I highly recommend them to any

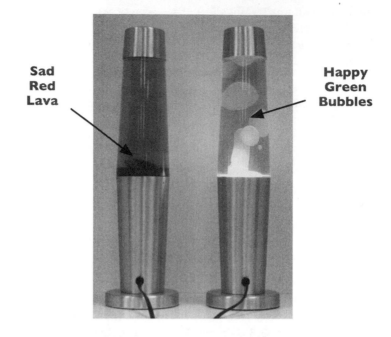

Sad Red Lava

Happy Green Bubbles

Figure 6.3: BUBBLES GREEN == BUILD IS CLEAN

software development organization that wants to make the most of their monitoring and feedback efforts. XFDs are inexpensive to build and operate, they add fun and color to the workspace, and most important they are effective in providing the team with feedback on key items and getting them to act upon it.

As we learned in Alberto's story, it's relatively easy and inexpensive to make build monitoring a spectator sport.[4] But don't stop there. Using similar techniques you can monitor *any* information that's valuable to your team.

---

[4]Alberto used a GPL Java library to interface with FireCracker, available at http://www.theprescotts.com/software/firecracker.

Mobile Visual Monitoring

The trouble with Lava Lamps is that you can't take them on the road with you. An alternative is to use an Ambient Orb.[5] It's a sphere the size of a softball that glows in a rainbow of colors. The cool part is that inside the orb is a wireless pager receiver. Simply plug the orb into a power source, and it receives wireless signals over a nationwide wireless network much like a cell phone or pager. For a small monthly fee you can purchase a premium account that lets you program how the orb changes color through the Ambient wireless network.

Imagine your project's Ambient Orb in a peaceful state glowing green. The next time your scheduled build runs, it fails. Behind the scenes a wireless packet is transmitted to your orb, and suddenly it turns red for everyone on the team to see!

6.3 Monitoring Your Java Process

Now that you have monitors in place for your build process, let's explore ways to use automation to monitor your deployed software.

We'll start with the simplest deployment: a long-running Java process. When you start it on a machine somewhere, it quietly goes to work offering some useful service. Let's assume that this service is shy, meaning that it doesn't offer a diagnostic interface or a user interface of any sort. Once it's started and you walk away, how will you know if it dies unexpectedly?

One cheap way to baby-sit a shy Java process is to start it under the watch of another tattletale process. The following Unix shell script does just that:

```
#!/bin/sh
while ! java com.pragprog.Main
do
  mail -s "Help Me!" 3035551212@mobile.att.net < email.txt
  sleep 60
done
```

monitors/launcher/launch.sh

---

[5]http://www.ambientdevices.com

The monitoring loop first starts the application by running the java command directly as the condition of the `while` loop (of course it could invoke any command or script that kick-starts your Java application). The loop then hangs waiting for the java command to exit. If the Java process exits with an exit code other than 0, then something went horribly wrong. This could happen because an exception came flying out of the main method or somebody "accidentally" killed the process.

When the process dies, it's time to call in the humans. The script sends a "Help Me!" text message to your cell phone or pager using the contents in email.txt as the message body. You could just as easily have it light up some visible object.

But it might be prudent to automatically restart the process before you've arrived on the scene. That's what the `while` loop buys us. The script sleeps for a minute just to avoid going berserk and then loops back to restart the process. If the process being monitored creates logs files, we don't want those files getting clobbered; it's important that the script save a time-stamped version of those files before restarting the process.

Simply by changing the way we start a Java process—putting it under the management of a process monitor—we're sure to know when it crashes.

6.4 Checking Up on Your Web Application

Web applications aren't so shy. Indeed, they have the capability of a remote diagnostic interface built right in. Consider, for example, the dreaded "404 Not Found" message. It's one not-so-subtle indication that your web application took an early vacation. An indication of an internal problem is seeing a default error page that includes an error message or (gasp!) an exception and its stack trace.

Here's the good news: If you can detect problems by looking at a web page, you can train a computer to watch for those same problems. Better yet, you don't pay a computer by the hour, so you can afford to have it *continuously* monitor web pages.

Writing a Screen Scraper

Writing a program that monitors a web page turns out to be remarkably easy if we choose the right tools. Sure, we could do this in Java, but it's overkill for this problem. You already have powerful HTML scrapers available to you: the curl and wget utilities. The following Unix shell script, checkurl.sh, will get the job done lickety-split:

```
#!/bin/sh
if [ $# -eq 0 ]
then
  echo "usage: checkurl.sh <url>"
  exit 1
fi
url=$1
outputfile="/tmp/test-$$.html"
to="3035551212@mobile.att.net"
subject="Uh oh!"
message=""

trap "rm -f $outputfile" 0

if curl -o $outputfile $url
then
  if grep -qiE "Error|Exception" $outputfile
  then
    message="Error or Exception"
  else
    exit 0  # success
  fi
else
  message="Unavailable"
fi
(cat << END_OF_MAIL
Sadly, $url isn't feeling well right now.

Diagnosis: $message

Thanks,
Your Humble Monitor
END_OF_MAIL
) | mail -s "$subject" "$to"
```

monitors/checkurl.sh

To check up on the *DMS* application, for example, run the script like this:

```
$ checkurl.sh http://xyz.com:8080/dms
```

The script uses curl to download the web page at the specified URL to a local temporary file. It then uses the ever-powerful grep command to search the downloaded page's contents for the presence of the word "Error" or "Exception." If the web page isn't found or if it's displaying either of those bad words, then your cell phone or pager receives the following text message:

```
Sadly, http://xyz.com:8080/dms isn't feeling well right now.
Diagnosis: Error or Exception
Thanks,
Your Humble Monitor
```

Scheduling a Checkup

Our freedom comes from monitors that run on a schedule. How often something is monitored is a decision we get to make based on how quickly we need to be notified of a problem.

After running the checkurl.sh script manually a time or two to make sure it works, you need to put it on a schedule. On Unix systems, the simplest scheduling tool is cron. To check every hour whether *DMS* is alive and well, for example, create a crontab entry like this:

```
0 * * * * $HOME/bin/checkurl.sh http://xyz.com:8080/dms
```

That's it! Now doesn't it feel good knowing this computer is watching your back? Admittedly, we haven't done anything fancy. It's just a cheap monitor that uses the good ol' fashioned screen scraping your father told you about. But it continues to pay you back by notifying you when problems occur.

Of course, you could noodle with this monitoring script for days or rewrite it in Ant, Ruby, Java, or whatever language makes you do a happy dance. But you don't have days to noodle with automation because you have to ship software, remember? So pick the simplest tools that get the job done, and then go back to preparing the next earth-shattering mega-release of your software.

6.5 Watching Log Files

Another way to monitor a Java application from the outside is by watching log files it updates. Many applications are already laced with logging statements ranging from harmless debugging information to end-of-the-world announcements. These are crude diagnostic interfaces, but they can be useful as early-warning detectors. That is, we can put a computer on guard watching logs for signs that our application has crashed or isn't feeling well and may crash.

Let's assume all error messages are being written to a local
error file. When that file is updated, it means your application
is crying for help. To constantly listen for those sounds, write
a program that monitors the error log file for changes.

We'll use Ruby just to illustrate that shell scripts aren't the
only way to create monitors. In the following Ruby program,
the watch method checks the specified file every minute. If the
modification time of the file has changed since the last time it
was checked, then the notify method is invoked.

```ruby
#!/usr/bin/env ruby
def watch(file)
  last_touched = File.mtime(file)
  loop do
    sleep 60
    current_time = File.mtime(file)
    if current_time != last_touched
      notify(file)
    end
    last_touched = current_time
  end
end
def notify(file)
  puts "#{file} was changed."
  # send an email, text message, etc.
end
if ARGV.empty?
  puts "Usage: filemonitor.rb <filename>"
  exit 1
end
watch(ARGV[0])
```

monitors/filemonitor.rb

To start monitoring the error log file, type

```
$ filemonitor.rb error.log
```

If the application you're monitoring happens to write all logging messages—from debug to fatal—in a single log file, then
the monitor will need to get a bit smarter. For example, it
might notify you when really bad things happen by searching
for new messages that include the word "FATAL."

The important thing to remember is that monitors are just
trip wires that cause some form of notification to be sent or
displayed. The notify method in this monitor, for example,
could do anything you want: send an email or text message,
broadcast a message to all users on the system, or change the
color of a visible object to bright red.

6.6 Monitoring with log4j

If an application is using a configurable logger such as log4j,[6] then we can do better than idly watch log files. Indeed, by simply changing an external configuration file, we can capture logging events as they happen inside the application.

How log4j Works

Say, for example, when running in production, your application logs only error and fatal messages. All other logging categories are disabled in this environment because of performance concerns. You've configured it this way by including the following line in the log4j.properties file:

```
log4j.logger.com.pragprog.dms=ERROR, logFile
```

Given this configuration, consider what happens when the following code is executed.

```
Logger logger = Logger.getLogger("com.pragprog.dms.Search");
logger.debug("Debug message");
logger.info("Info message");
logger.warn("Warning message");
logger.error("Error messsage");
logger.fatal("Fatal message");
```

It first gets an instance of a Logger by requesting a logger named com.pragprog.dms.Search. Because there's no logger by that exact name in the configuration, so it returns the Logger instance matching the com.pragprog.dms prefix. Since that logger is assigned a level of ERROR, it will log only messages at that level or higher: ERROR or FATAL. Therefore, it logs only the messages passed to the error and fatal methods.

appenders Loggers send their messages to all registered destinations, called *appenders*. In this case, the only appender is log-File, which is configured to write log messages to a file called error.log. Thus, when the program is run, the following messages are logged to the error log file:

```
ERROR - Error messsage
FATAL - Fatal message
```

---

[6]http://logging.apache.org/log4j

Plugging In a Monitoring Appender

In addition to spooling all error and fatal message to an error log file, we'd like to create our own monitor for those logging events.

log4j allows multiple appenders to be registered for each logger. It's distributed with a variety of prebuilt appenders to send logging messages to the console, a file, a socket, email addresses, the Unix Syslog daemon, the NT Event logger, or asynchronously to a JMS destination. If you'd like your messages color coded on a GUI display, you could run Chainsaw— a GUI-based log viewer which can monitor logging events in remote applications through a socket.

But if the stock appenders aren't enough, you can write a custom log4j appender that opens the door for just about any type of monitoring. The easiest way to write a custom appender is to create a class that extends AppenderSkeleton.

```
package com.pragprog.dms;
import org.apache.log4j.AppenderSkeleton;
import org.apache.log4j.spi.LoggingEvent;
public class MonitoringAppender extends AppenderSkeleton {
  protected void append(LoggingEvent event) {
    // send or display notification
  }
  public boolean requiresLayout() {
    return false;
  }
  public void close() { }
}
```

monitors/logger/MonitoringAppender.java

The append method is called for all logging events destined for the MonitoringAppender. Let's say you want this appender to receive the same logging messages as the error log file: error and fatal messages only. Simply register the appender with the logger by updating the log4j.properties file.

```
log4j.logger.com.pragprog.dms=ERROR, logFile, monitor
log4j.appender.monitor=com.pragprog.dms.MonitoringAppender
```

This gives us a way to monitor the application for problems without having to watch the log file directly. We could implement the append method of the MonitoringAppender to send a notification by any means or turn on a visual device. Again, this monitor serves merely as a trip wire. The notification mechanism we use is based on the severity of the problem.

Just how far can you take logger-based monitoring? For one answer to that question, let's now turn our attention to a project where bugs can't hide.[7]

Automatic Crash Reporting
by Bob Lee, http://crazybob.org

It seems that more often than not, logging fails to garner the respect it deserves. Many applications weave megabytes of useful debug information from a combination of thousands of successful and failed requests into a single log file. Tools help filter the result to some degree but can't help much when the production application foregoes debug-level logging for the sake of performance. How many times have you troubleshot a production issue sans adequate information?

My current web application made do during development with a simple default error page that printed the exception stack trace to the browser. Testers would copy the stack trace and enter a short description into Bugzilla. In the past, when the production deadline rolled around, we would typically modify the error handler to display a generic error message and unique ID in place of the stack trace and fire off an email to an administrator. This time we decided to turn things up a notch. First, throwing away useful debug-level log messages seemed like an enormous waste. If dumping the messages from separate requests to one place produces a bottleneck, why not keep them separate? Second, filing bugs and filtering out duplicates struck me as unnecessarily rote. How could we better automate the process?

So I built a crash reporting framework (nicknamed "Bobzilla" by a co-worker). The simple implementation does not impact application code; we combine a custom Servlet filter and a custom log4j appender to capture the log messages for the scope of a web request in a thread-local buffer. When the filter catches an exception, it creates a new bug in Bugzilla and uses the log messages leading up to the exception and the exception's stack trace as the bug description.

Integrating with Bugzilla proved easier than we expected. Tired of waiting for permission to directly access the Bugzilla

---

[7]This story first appeared on http://java.net.

database, I decided to post bugs directly to the Bugzilla web application. I discovered through experimentation that Bugzilla lets you pass the user ID and password along with the rest of the parameters, so authentication was a snap. Integration amounted to looking at the HTML source for the "New Bug" page to see what parameters it passed in and duplicating the effort using a Java URLConnection.

We filter out duplicate exceptions by hashing the stack trace. Unfortunately, even after some experimentation and tweaking, a couple duplicates still make it through; however, any further filtering must be application specific and would require more development effort than simply invalidating duplicate bugs by hand. We're still much better off than where we started.

With "Bobzilla" in place for a few weeks now, the turnaround time for addressing bugs has dropped considerably, testers focus more time identifying functionality issues, fewer problems slip through the cracks, we collect debug level messages in production with no performance penalty, and I no longer waste time tailing logs and filtering the noise caused by ten concurrent requests.

This is a clever and efficient way to automatically turn exceptions into trackable issues. The program in the story is an in-house hosted application, but this technique could be used by any application with network access. Those applications just need a way to "phone home" when a problem occurs.

6.7 Building Trip Wires with RSS

As you learn more about the kinds of things worth monitoring in your application, you can add special monitoring trip wires. These might be important events, but you don't need to get immediate notification when they happen.

For example, say you'd like to know when somebody orders five or more books. Perhaps you want to send them a box of chocolates. With log4j you might use a logger called sales and log a significant book order event like this:

```
Logger logger = Logger.getLogger("sales");
logger.info("Joe (joe@xyz.com) ordered 10 books!");
```

When this event happens, you don't want to have to go searching through a log file or your email inbox. You'd like the notification pushed to you via RSS so that you have a history of all big orders in one RSS feed. That way everyone who has a vested interest in book sales can watch the same feed.

To do that, write a custom log4j appender called RSSAppender, for example. Then change the log4j.properties file to add a new logger called `sales` that uses this new RSSAppender as its destination.

```
log4j.logger.sales=INFO, rss
log4j.appender.rss=com.pragprog.RSSAppender
```

This now means that the appender named `rss` is assigned to the logger named `sales` with a logging level of INFO or higher. And once the sales-related logging statements have been inserted into the code, you can selectively enable or disable them level by level by changing the log4j.properties file.

The append method of the RSSAppender would need to make a new RSS item for each logging message it receives. Here's an example RSS feed with two items:

```
<?xml version="1.0" encoding="iso-8859-1" ?>
<rss version="0.91">
<channel>
  <title>Sales Info</title>
  <description>Important sales events.</description>
  <language>en-us</language>
  <item>
    <title>Big Order</title>
    <description>
      Joe (joe@xyz.com) ordered 10 books!
    </description>
  </item>
  <item>
    <title>One-Millionth Customer</title>
    <description>
      Sally (sally@xyz.com) just broke the one-million mark!
    </description>
  </item>
</channel>
</rss>
```

monitors/rss/sales.rss

Then anyone with access to that RSS file could listen to sales events by pointing their RSS reader to the RSS feed. Figure 6.4 on the next page shows the sales information in the NetNewsWire reader. So, monitoring can be more than waiting for something bad to happen. Indeed, it can also be used to notify us of something good in a timely way.

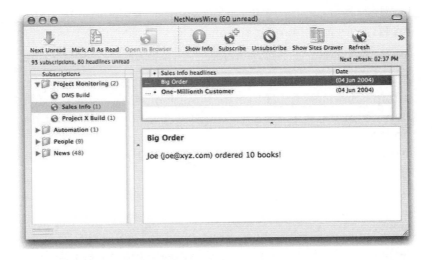

Figure 6.4: SALES INFORMATION VIA RSS

6.8 Monitoring Health with a Debug Command

When a remote application is showing signs of being ill, it would be helpful if we could ask it where it hurts. To do that, create an internal debug command that dumps the application's health on demand. The output might include

- JVM statistics
- The last error message logged
- Number of concurrent users on the system
- Open database connections vs. connection pool size
- Average response time of a key web page

One way to get a debug dump is to run a command-line program that connects to a remote program and asks for a report. However, a web interface offers a powerful alternative.

Asking a Web Server

HTTP is a ubiquitous and convenient interface protocol that works even through most firewalls. If an application is running in a web server, then you can get information about it remotely by issuing HTTP requests. For example, to generate a debug dump of the *DMS* application as it's running, send it an HTTP request similar to this:

```
http://xyz.com:8080/dms/debugdump
```

That URL would map to some resource that generates a debug dump showing an arbitrary amount of diagnostic information about the application. To get a diagnostic report, either browse to that URL or run a screen scraper that sends the request programmatically and checks the response for telltale signs of a problem.

This monitoring technique is powerful enough that you might want to consider embedding a web server in remote applications that aren't already running inside a web server. That is, rather than building a remote diagnostic interface, just bring all the power of HTTP right to the application.

Embedding a web server might involve writing a bare-bones web server or just using something like Jetty:[8] a small, fast, free, and embeddable HTTP server and servlet container. Let's see just how easy Jetty is to embed:

```java
import org.mortbay.http.HttpServer;
import org.mortbay.jetty.servlet.ServletHandler;
public class WebServer {
  public static void main(String[] args) throws Exception {
    HttpServer server = new HttpServer();
    server.addListener("8080");
    ServletHandler handler = new ServletHandler();
    handler.addServlet("DebugDumpServlet", "/debugdump/*",
      "com.pragprog.DebugDumpServlet");
    server.getContext("/").addHandler(handler);
    server.start();
  }
}
```

Running that minimal code starts an HTTP server on port 8080 with the DebugDumpServlet mapped to the /debugdump/ path. Serving static content from a directory is even easier.

6.9 Creating a Crash Report

Sometimes, applications crash. When they do, we'll want to do a postmortem analysis to find out what went wrong in

---

[8]http://jetty.mortbay.org

hopes of preventing it from happening again. Log files can hold some of the clues, but they can be too much information to wade through and they're usually just one piece of the puzzle.

Go a step further by writing a simple script or batch file that knows how to collect just the right amount of evidence from various sources, including

- The last *x* number of messages in the log file
- The version of the application
- The operating system and JVM version
- Key environment variables and system properties
- Names of other running processes

When a user experiences a crash, they run the script and send you the resulting crash report. Better yet, the application could automatically create the crash report and display it in a dialog box or an HTML form. The user then gets a chance to review the crash report before pushing the button that submits it over the web to your technical support server. Taking a lesson from the automatic crash reporting story previously, that server could record the crash as a new bug in your issue-tracking database.

6.10 3-2-1...

My friend Bryce Unruh is a rocket scientist, literally. His team designs hardware and embedded software for science-gathering instruments that fly aboard satellites out in space. Launching their product consists of installing the software on the hardware, strapping the hardware to a four-story rocket, and lighting the fuse.

OK, it's slightly more complicated than that. The result, however, is the same: Successfully deploying their product puts it far out of their reach in an environment less hospitable than your average server room. And failure is a *very* expensive option. So once their handiwork is in orbit, they need to continuously monitor its health as a heads-up for scheduling preventative maintenance.

As you can imagine, they're busy folk, and they don't have time to sit around channel-surfing through all the spacecraft's data waiting for a problem. They're much too busy for that sort of active monitoring. At any given time, the team may have several systems deployed high above their heads while they're hard at work on the next stellar system. So how can they possibly stay on top of everything in the universe? As Bryce explains in the following story, they use automation to turn science fiction into science fact:

A Story from Outer Space

by Bryce Unruh, Ball Aerospace & Technologies Corp

Our team was responsible for maintaining the flight software for two instruments on the Spitzer Space Telescope: one of NASA's Great Observatories currently in its first year of a five-plus year mission.

Because of the telescope's unique orbit (earth trailing, heliocentric) and communication constraints with the Deep Space Network, contact windows between the ground stations and the telescope occur at about 12-hour intervals. During these contacts, science and engineering data are transmitted from the observatory. Hundreds of telemetry items are transmitted during this downlink, and it is crucial that our team be notified immediately if certain values are out of limit.

The out-of-limit channels are identified by an automatic alarm notification system, and a text message is sent to everyone on our team. A simple message is sent to our text pagers that includes the telemetry channel, alarm value, time stamp, and spacecraft ID. The team member on call then looks up the telemetry channel in our database, assesses the severity of the situation, and takes appropriate action.

We also have another method of capturing less obvious metrics on our software's performance. Our software is written to detect errors that occur during instrument operation. These errors are written to an internal error buffer in memory. Each entry contains the error ID, error parameter, and time stamp. When the instrument is commanded to turn off, an on-board spacecraft sequence of commands dumps the memory area which includes the error buffers. Ground software has been written to take this memory dump data and send the team a summary of errors that occurred during the instrument campaign.

As we saw in Bryce's down-to-earth story, automated monitoring can help you gather important information about your deployed software without you having to continuously ask it how it's feeling. When it requires attention, it lets you know. In the meantime, you're free to go merrily about your terrestrial business.

Thankfully, *you* don't have to be a rocket scientist or have an astronomical budget to enjoy the benefits of automated monitoring. Asynchronous communication with email, cell phones, and pagers has never been easier. The techniques we've used in this chapter can be applied to monitoring all kinds of stuff.

6.11 Automate!

So, now we've finished. We've put together repeatable builds and arranged for them to be run automatically. We've created installers that let us deploy our applications at the push of a button and written tests that allow those installations to be tested once they arrive on a client's system. And, just because things sometimes go wrong, we've arranged for all these steps to notify us of problems, whereever we are in the world.

And all of this is being done automatically, without any intervention on our part. That's sweet—the machines are doing all the boring work for us. Now we can get down to coding the interesting stuff....

Appendix A

Resources

A.1 On the Web

Ant . . . . http://ant.apache.org
A specialized build tool for Java that's powerful, portable, extensible, and integrated into many Java IDEs.

Anthill . . . . http://www.urbancode.com/projects/anthill
An Ant build scheduler similar to CruiseControl that runs inside of a Servlet container.

CruiseControl . . . . . . http://cruisecontrol.sourceforge.net
An application and extensible framework for a continuous build process. It includes plug-ins for email notification, version control systems, and Ant and Maven integration.

CVS . . . . http://cvshome.org
A widely used, open-source version control system.

Cygwin . . . . http://www.cygwin.com
A POSIX emulation library for Windows.

Groovy . . . . http://groovy.codehaus.org
A dynamic language with Java-like syntax that runs on the Java platform.

Java Web Start . . .
. . . http://java.sun.com/products/javawebstart
A web-based deployment and auto-update technology bundled in newer versions of Java.

Jetty . . . . http://jetty.mortbay.org/jetty
An embeddable web server and Servlet container.

JUnit . . . . http://junit.org
The de facto standard unit testing tool for Java.

log4j . . . . `http://logging.apache.org/log4j`
A highly configurable logging framework for Java.

NSIS . . . . `http://nsis.sourceforge.net`
The Nullsoft Scriptable Install System (NSIS) is a free installer and uninstaller for Windows.

Pragmatic Automation . . . `http://pragmaticautomation.com`
The companion web site for this book where you'll find fresh news, stories, and content related to all sorts of project automation. Got an automation story from your project? Submit it here.

Pragmatic Programming . . .
. . . `http://www.pragmaticprogrammer.com`
The Pragmatic Programmer's home page, where you'll find links to the Pragmatic Bookshelf titles (including this book), along with information for developers and managers.

A.2 Bibliography

[HL02]   Erik Hatcher and Steve Loughran. *Java Development with Ant.* Manning Publications Co., Greenwich, CT, 2002.

[HT00]   Andrew Hunt and David Thomas. *The Pragmatic Programmer: From Journeyman to Master.* Addison-Wesley, Reading, MA, 2000.

[HT03]   Andrew Hunt and David Thomas. *Pragmatic Unit Testing In Java with JUnit.* The Pragmatic Programmers, LLC, Raleigh, NC, and Dallas, TX, 2003.

[TH03]   David Thomas and Andrew Hunt. *Pragmatic Version Control Using CVS.* The Pragmatic Programmers, LLC, Raleigh, NC, and Dallas, TX, 2003.

Pragmatic Project Automation: Summary

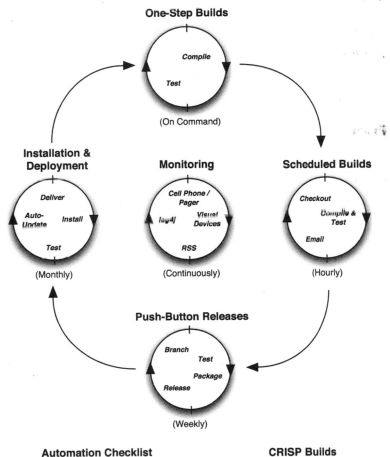

One-Step Builds
Compile
Test
(On Command)

Installation & Deployment
Deliver
Auto-Update
Install
Test
(Monthly)

Monitoring
Cell Phone / Pager
[lava]
Visual Devices
RSS
(Continuously)

Scheduled Builds
Checkout
Compile & Test
Email
(Hourly)

Push-Button Releases
Branch
Test
Package
Release
(Weekly)

Automation Checklist

☐ Create a one-step build process

☐ Build on a frequent schedule

☐ Write branch and release scripts

☐ Create an installer/deployer

☐ Monitor builds and applications

☐ Review and revise

CRISP Builds

Complete

Repeatable

Informative

Schedulable

Portable

http://www.pragmaticprogrammer.com/sk/auto

Index

Pragmatic Starter Kit

Version Control. **Unit Testing**. **Project Automation**. Three great titles, one objective. To get you up to speed with the essentials for successful project development. Keep your source under control, your bugs in check, and your process repeatable with these three concise, readable books from The Pragmatic Bookshelf.

Visit Us Online

Project Automation Home Page
pragmaticprogrammer.com/sk/auto
Source code from this book, errata, and other resources. Come give us feedback, too!

Register for Updates
pragmaticprogrammer.com/updates
Be notified when updates and new books become available.

Join the Community
pragmaticprogrammer.com/community
Read our weblogs, join our online discussions, participate in our mailing list, interact with our wiki, and benefit from the experience of other Pragmatic Programmers.

New and Noteworthy
pragmaticprogrammer.com/news
Check out the latest pragmatic developments in the news.

Save on the PDF

Save more than 60% on the PDF version of this book. Owning the paper version of this book entitles you to purchase the PDF version for only $7.50 (regularly $20.00). That's a saving of more than 60%. The PDF is great for carrying around on your laptop. It's hyperlinked, has color, and is fully searchable. Buy it now at pragmaticprogrammer.com/coupon

Contact Us

Phone Orders:	1-800-699-PROG (+1 919 847 3884)
Online Orders:	www.pragmaticprogrammer.com/catalog
Customer Service:	orders@pragmaticprogrammer.com
Non-English Versions:	translations@pragmaticprogrammer.com
Pragmatic Teaching:	academic@pragmaticprogrammer.com
Author Proposals:	proposals@pragmaticprogrammer.com